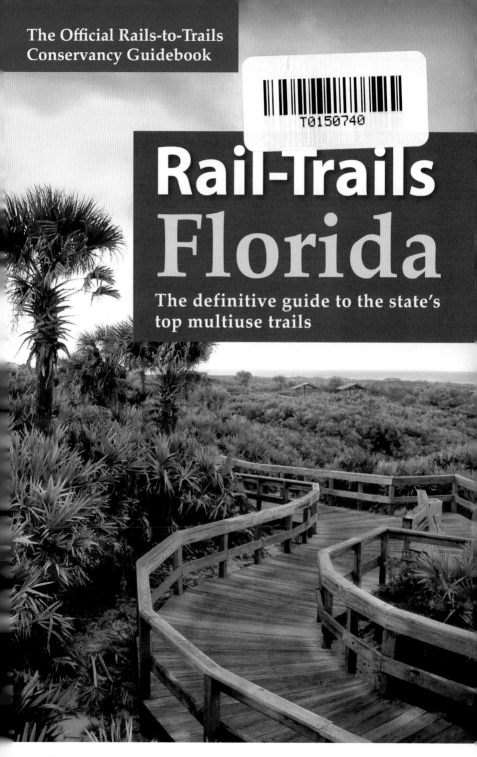

The Official Rails-to-Trails
Conservancy Guidebook

Rail-Trails
Florida

The definitive guide to the state's
top multiuse trails

WILDERNESS PRESS ... *on the trail since 1967*

Rail-Trails: Florida

1st edition, 5th printing 2021
Copyright © 2016 by Rails-to-Trails Conservancy
All cover and interior photographs © Rails-to-Trails Conservancy

Maps: Lohnes+Wright; map data courtesy of Environmental Systems Research Institute
Cover design: Scott McGrew
Book design: Annie Long

Library of Congress Cataloging-in-Publication Data

Names: Rails-to-Trails Conservancy.
Title: Rail-trails : Florida.
Description: Birmingham, AL : Wilderness Press, [2016] | At head of title: The Official
    Rails-to-Trails Conservancy Guidebook. | "Distributed by Publishers Group West"—T.p.
    verso. | Includes bibliographical references and index.
Identifiers: LCCN 2016000572 (print) | LCCN 2016007186 (ebook) | ISBN
    9780899978192 (alk. paper) | ISBN 9780899978208 (eBook) | ISBN 9780899978208 ()
Subjects: LCSH: Rail-trails—Florida—Guidebooks. | Outdoor recreation—Florida—
    Guidebooks. | Florida—Guidebooks.
Classification: LCC GV191.42.F6 R35 2016 (print) | LCC GV191.42.F6 (ebook) | DDC
    796.509759—dc23
LC record available at http://lccn.loc.gov/2016000572

Manufactured in China

Published by: **WILDERNESS PRESS**
An imprint of AdventureKEEN
2204 First Ave. S, Ste. 102
Birmingham, AL 35233
800-678-7008; fax (877) 374-9016

Visit wildernesspress.com for a complete listing of our books and for ordering information. Contact us at our website, at facebook.com/wildernesspress1967, or at twitter.com
/wilderness1967 with questions or comments. To find out more about who we are and
what we're doing, visit blog.wildernesspress.com.

Distributed by Publishers Group West

Front and back covers: Ponce Inlet Trail (see page 114); photographed by Chris Crowley

SAFETY NOTICE: Although Wilderness Press and Rails-to-Trails Conservancy have
made every attempt to ensure that the information in this book is accurate at press time,
they are not responsible for any loss, damage, injury, or inconvenience that may occur to
anyone while using this book. You are responsible for your own safety and health while in
the wilderness. The fact that a trail is described in this book does not mean that it will be
safe for you. Be aware that trail conditions can change from day to day. Always check local
conditions, know your own limitations, and consult a map.

About Rails-to-Trails Conservancy

Headquartered in Washington, D.C., Rails-to-Trails Conservancy (RTC) is a nonprofit organization dedicated to creating a nationwide network of trails from former rail lines and connecting corridors to build healthier places for healthier people.

Railways helped build America. Spanning from coast to coast, these ribbons of steel linked people, communities, and enterprises, spurring commerce and forging a single nation that bridges a continent. But in recent decades, many of these routes have fallen into disuse, severing communal ties that helped bind Americans together.

When RTC opened its doors in 1986, the rail-trail movement was in its infancy. Though there were some 250 known miles of open rail-trails in the United States, most projects focused on single, linear routes in rural areas, created for recreation and conservation. RTC sought broader protection for the unused corridors, incorporating rural, suburban, and urban routes.

Year after year, RTC's efforts to protect and align public funding with trail building created an environment that allowed trail advocates in communities across the country to initiate trail projects. These ever-growing ranks of trail professionals, volunteers, and RTC supporters have built momentum for the national rail-trails movement. As the number of supporters multiplied, so did the rail-trails.

Americans now enjoy more than 22,000 miles of open rail-trails; as they flock to the trails to connect with family members and friends, enjoy nature, and get to places in their local neighborhoods and beyond, their economic prosperity, health, and overall well-being continue to flourish.

A signature endeavor of RTC is **TrailLink.com,** America's portal to these rail-trails, as well as other multiuse trails. When RTC launched **TrailLink.com** in 2000, our organization was one of the first to compile such detailed trail information on a national scale. Today, the website continues to play a critical role in both encouraging and satisfying the country's growing need for opportunities to ride, walk, skate, or run for recreation or transportation. This free trail-finder database—which includes detailed descriptions, interactive maps, photo galleries, and firsthand ratings and reviews—can be used as a companion resource to the trails in this guidebook.

The national voice for more than 160,000 members and supporters, RTC is committed to ensuring a better future for America made possible by trails and the connections they inspire. Learn more at **railstotrails.org.**

The Old Cutler Trail passes through a tree-lined neighborhood in Coral Gables (see page 105).

Table of Contents

Foreword

For those of you who have already experienced the sheer enjoyment and freedom of riding on a rail-trail, welcome back. You'll find *Rail-Trails: Florida* to be a useful and fun guide to your favorite trails, as well as an introduction to pathways you have yet to travel.

For readers who are discovering for the first time the adventures possible on a rail-trail, thank you for joining the rail-trail movement. Since 1986, Rails-to-Trails Conservancy has been the leading supporter and defender of these priceless public corridors. We are excited to bring you *Rail-Trails: Florida* so you, too, can enjoy some of this state's rail-trails and multiuse trails. These hiking and biking trails are ideal ways to connect with your community, with nature, and with your friends and family.

I've found that trails have a way of bringing people together, and as you'll see from this book, you have opportunities in every city you visit to get on a great trail. Whether you're looking for a place to exercise, explore, commute, or play, there is a trail in this book for you.

So I invite you to sit back, relax, pick a trail that piques your interest, and then get out, get active, and have some fun. I'll be out on the trails too, so be sure to wave as you go by.

Happy trails,
Keith Laughlin, President
Rails-to-Trails Conservancy

Stop and take in the view at one of several crossings over the Ten Mile Canal in Fort Myers along the John Yarbrough Linear Park Trail (see page 71).

Acknowledgments

Many thanks to the following contributors and to all the trail managers we called on for assistance to ensure the maps, photographs, and trail descriptions are as accurate as possible:

Milo Bateman	Barry Bergman
Jim Brown	Ken Bryan
Ryan Cree	Cindy Dickerson
Brian Gerhardstein	Eli Griffen
Katie Harris	Amy Kapp
Kesi Marcus	Eric Oberg
Jon Rayer	Anya Saretzky
Leeann Sinpatanasakul	Laura Stark

Winter Garden's West Orange Trail at night (see page 164)

Introduction

Of the more than 1,900 rail-trails across the United States, 48 are located in the state of Florida. Spanning waterways, urban and rural areas, and some of Florida's most unique terrain, these pathways help preserve and pay homage to the rich history of a state known for its marine life, fishing and agricultural industries, and beautiful islands and beaches.

Highlighted in this guide are 29 rail-trails and 23 multiuse trails of all shapes and sizes, running along canals and waterways and through a diverse set of landscapes—including pine and mangrove forest, swamp, beach, and farm pasture—on some of the flattest and lowest-sea-level geography in the United States. Paleo-Indians are thought to have first inhabited Florida approximately 12,000 years ago, and post-Archaic tribes arrived about 3,000 years ago. Their legacy lives on in the names of many trails (for example: Timucuan, Withlacoochee, and Seminole). Florida was the first part of the continental United States ever to be visited by Europeans; in fact, the 3.5-mile Ponce Inlet Trail bears the name of the first explorer, Juan Ponce de León, as well as the state's tallest lighthouse.

The Florida Keys Overseas Heritage Trail offers a quintessential Florida Keys experience as it traverses 106.5 miles from Key Largo to Key West, past 10 state parks, on the former historic Overseas Railroad. For an urban experience, try the 44.3-mile Fred Marquis Pinellas Trail, which stretches along the Gulf of Mexico from St. Petersburg to Tarpon Springs, connecting county parks, coastal areas, and communities. The 20.5-mile Tallahassee–St. Marks Historic Railroad State Trail, which follows the state's oldest railroad corridor, offers a variety of environments—from urban to remote—between its starting point near Florida State University and its endpoint at the popular St. Mark's waterfront and the 500,000-acre San Marcos de Apalache Historic State Park.

No matter which route in *Rail-Trails: Florida* you decide to try, you'll be touching on the heart of the community that helped build it and the unique history and geography it encapsulates.

What Is a Rail-Trail?

Rail-trails are multiuse public paths built along former railroad corridors. Most often flat or following a gentle grade, they are suited to walking, running, cycling, mountain biking, in-line skating, cross-country skiing, horseback riding, and wheelchair use. Since the 1960s, Americans have created more than 22,000 miles of rail-trails throughout the country.

These extremely popular recreation and transportation corridors traverse urban, suburban, and rural landscapes. Many preserve historic landmarks, while others serve as wildlife conservation corridors, linking isolated parks and establishing greenways in developed areas. Rail-trails also stimulate local economies by boosting tourism and promoting trailside businesses.

What Is a Rail-with-Trail?

A rail-with-trail is a public path that parallels a still-active rail line. Some run adjacent to high-speed, scheduled trains, often linking public transportation stations, while others follow tourist routes and slow-moving excursion trains. Many share an easement, separated from the rails by extensive fencing. More than 250 rails-with-trails exist in the United States.

How to Use This Book

Rail-Trails: Florida provides the information you'll need to plan a rewarding trail trek. With words to inspire you and maps to chart your path, it makes choosing the best route a breeze. Following are some of the highlights.

Maps

You'll find two levels of maps in this book: a **state locator map** and **detailed trail maps.**

Use these maps to find the trails nearest you, or select several neighboring trails and plan a weekend hiking or biking excursion. Once you find a trail on the state locator map, simply flip to that trail's detail page for a full description. Accompanying trail maps mark each route's access roads, trailheads, parking areas, restrooms, and other defining features.

Key to Map Icons

Parking

Drinking water

Restrooms

Trail Descriptions

Trails are listed in alphabetical order. Each description leads off with a set of summary information, including trail endpoints and mileage, a roughness index, the trail surface, and possible uses.

The map and summary information list the trail endpoints (a city, street, or more specific location) with suggested points from which to start and finish. Additional access points are marked on the maps and mentioned in the trail descriptions. The maps and descriptions also highlight available amenities, including parking and restrooms, as well as such area attractions as services, museums, parks, and stadiums. Trail length is listed in miles.

Each trail bears a **roughness index** rating from 1 to 3. A rating of 1 indicates a smooth, level surface that is accessible to users of all ages and abilities. A 2 rating means the surface may be loose and/or uneven and could pose a problem for road bikes and wheelchairs. A 3 rating suggests a rough surface that is recommended only for mountain bikers and hikers. Surfaces can range from asphalt or concrete to ballast, boardwalk, cinder, crushed stone, gravel, grass, dirt, sand, and/or wood chips. Where relevant, trail descriptions address alternating surface conditions.

All trails are open to pedestrians, and most allow bicycles, except where noted in the trail summary or description. The summary also indicates wheelchair access. Other possible uses include in-line skating, mountain biking, hiking, horseback riding, fishing, and cross-country skiing. While most trails are off-limits to motor vehicles, some local trail organizations do allow all-terrain vehicles (ATVs).

Trail descriptions themselves suggest an ideal itinerary for each route, including the best parking areas and access points, where to begin, your direction of travel, and any highlights along the way. Following each description are directions to the recommended trailheads.

Each trail description also lists a local website for further information. Be sure to visit these websites in advance for updates and current conditions. **TrailLink.com** is another great resource for updated content on the trails in this guidebook.

Trail Use

Rail-trails are popular destinations for a range of users, often making them busy places to enjoy the outdoors. Following basic trail etiquette and safety guidelines will make your experience more pleasant.

Keep to the right, except when passing.

Pass on the left, and give a clear, audible warning: "Passing on your left."

Be aware of other trail users, particularly around corners and blind spots, and be especially careful when entering a trail, changing direction, or passing so that you don't collide with traffic.

Respect wildlife and public and private property; leave no trace and take out litter.

Control your speed, especially near pedestrians, playgrounds, and heavily congested areas.

Travel single file. Cyclists and pedestrians should ride or walk single file in congested areas or areas with reduced visibility.

Cross carefully at intersections; always look both ways and yield to through traffic. Pedestrians have the right-of-way.

Keep one ear open and volume low on portable listening devices to increase your awareness of your surroundings.

Wear a helmet and other safety gear if you're cycling or in-line skating.

Consider visibility. Wear reflective clothing, use bicycle lights, or bring flashlights or helmet-mounted lights for tunnel passages or twilight excursions.

Keep moving, and don't block the trail. When taking a rest, turn off the trail to the right. Groups should avoid congregating on or blocking the trails. If you have an accident on the trail, move to the right as soon as possible.

Bicyclists yield to all other trail users. Pedestrians yield to horses. If in doubt, yield to all other trail users.

Dogs are permitted on most trails, but some trails through parks, wildlife refuges, or other sensitive areas may not allow pets; it's best to check the trail website before your visit. If pets are permitted, keep your dog on a short leash and under your control at all times. Dispose of dog waste in a designated trash receptacle.

Teach your children these trail essentials, and be especially diligent to keep them out of faster-moving trail traffic.

Be prepared, especially on long-distance rural trails. Bring water, snacks, maps, a light source, matches, sunscreen, and other equipment you may need. Because some areas may not have good reception for mobile phones, know where you're going, and tell someone else your plan.

Key to Trail Use

cycling

in-line skating

fishing

wheelchair access

horseback riding

mountain biking

walking

Learn More

To learn about additional rail-trails in your area or to plan a trip to an area beyond the scope of this book, visit Rails-to-Trails Conservancy's trail-finder website, **TrailLink.com,** a free resource with information on more than 30,000 miles of trails nationwide.

Florida

rails-to-trails
conservancy

ATLANTIC OCEAN

GEORGIA

FLORIDA

Gulf of Mexico

NEW ORLEANS
PENSACOLA
TALLAHASSEE
JACKSONVILLE
GAINESVILLE
ORLANDO
TAMPA
MIAMI

N

0 — 100 miles

1	Amelia Island Trail
2	Atlantic Greenway (East Coast Greenway)
3	Auburndale TECO Trail
4	Black Creek Trail (Miami-Dade)
5	Blackwater Heritage State Trail
6	Blountstown Greenway Bike Path
7	Boca Grande Bike Path
8	Cady Way Trail
9	Courtney Campbell Trail
10	Cross Seminole Trail
11	East Central Regional Rail Trail
12	El Rio Trail
13	Florida Keys Overseas Heritage Trail
14	Fort Fraser Trail
15	Fred Marquis Pinellas Trail
16	Gainesville-Hawthorne State Trail
17	General James A. Van Fleet State Trail
18	Gordon River Greenway
19	Historic Jungle Trail
20	Jacksonville-Baldwin Rail-Trail
21	John Yarbrough Linear Park Trail
22	Lake Apopka Loop Trail
23	Lake Okeechobee Scenic Trail (LOST)
24	Legacy Trail
25	Lehigh Greenway Rail Trail
26	Little Econ Greenway
27	M-Path Trail
28	Nature Coast State Trail
29	New River Greenway
30	North Bay Trail
31	Ocean Boulevard Path
32	Old Cutler Trail
33	Palatka–Lake Butler State Trail
34	Palatka–St. Augustine State Trail
35	Ponce Inlet Trail
36	Ream Wilson Clearwater Trail
37	Rickenbacker Trail
38	Robbins Vista View Trail
39	Sanibel Island Shared-Use Paths
40	Seminole Wekiva Trail
41	Snake Creek Trail
42	South Lake and Lake Minneola Scenic Trail
43	Spring to Spring Trail
44	St. George Island Bike Path
45	Suncoast Trail
46	Tallahassee–St. Marks Historic Railroad State Trail
47	Timucuan Trail
48	Upper Tampa Bay Trail
49	Waldo Road Greenway–Depot Avenue Rail-Trail–Kermit Sigmon Bike Trail
50	West Orange Trail
51	Withlacoochee Bay Trail
52	Withlacoochee State Trail

Florida

The Cady Way Trail offers a pleasant stroll through Orlando (see page 29).

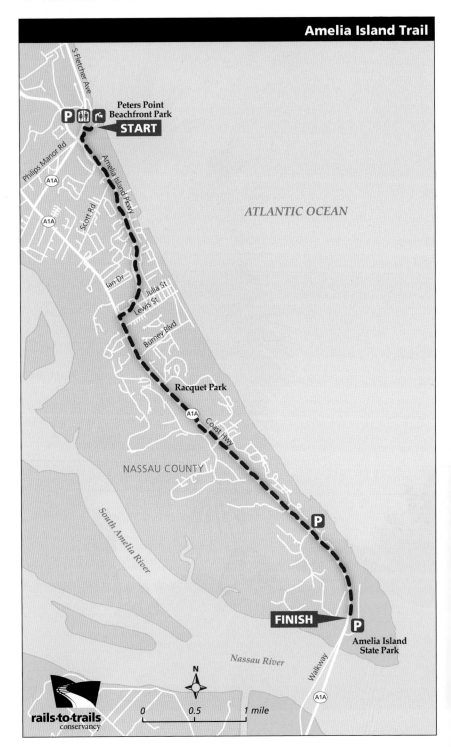

Amelia Island Trail

This 5.7-mile rail-trail parallels the southern shoreline of Amelia Island, a member of the Sea Island chain along Florida's northeast coast that boasts beaches, a variety of recreation options, and charismatic towns.

Peters Point Beachfront Park—the northern terminus of the trail—provides ample parking, restrooms, and picnic tables, making it an ideal starting point. The trail follows FL A1A for almost its entire length, but most of the trail is buffered from road noise by a screen of green, including live oaks cloaked in Spanish moss. Snakes and lizards are common sightings along the relatively straight, flat route, and plant enthusiasts will love the variety of foliage lining the way. Access to Amelia Island beaches is available at both the northern trailhead and the southern terminus at Amelia Island State Park, and you'll find parking at both endpoints, as well as close to the southern terminus, just north of Long Point Drive.

The flora of northern Florida—including the pretty dwarf palmetto—are on full display along the Amelia Island Trail.

Location
Nassau

Endpoints
Peters Point Beachfront Park at FL A1A and Amelia Island Pkwy. to Amelia Island State Park at FL A1A and Nassau Sound (Fernandina Beach)

Mileage
5.7

Type
Greenway/Non-Rail-Trail

Roughness Index
1

Surface
Asphalt

Be sure to pack a swimsuit and sunscreen for some rest and respite at the park. Wildlife sightings are common along the shore, so keep your eyes peeled and a camera at the ready. If you have more time, consider a trip along the Timucuan Island Trail, which is just south of Amelia Island, separated by the Nassau Sound.

CONTACT: ameliaislandtrail.org

DIRECTIONS

To reach the Peters Point Beachfront Park trailhead from I-95, take Exit 373 for FL 200/FL A1A toward Callahan/Fernandina Beach. Head east on FL 200/FL A1A S./The Buccaneer Trail (signs for FL 200 E./Yulee/Amelia Island/Fernandina Beach). Follow the road 11.3 miles through Yulee and O'Neil and across St. Marys River to Amelia Island. Turn right onto Amelia Island Pkwy., and go 3.2 miles (after 1.5 miles, you'll take the first exit at the traffic circle to stay on the parkway another 1.7 miles). Turn left onto FL A1A, and then immediately turn right onto Peters Point Road. The trailhead is to your right at the intersection of Peters Point Road and Carlton Dunes Drive. You'll find parking just ahead and to your left at Peters Point Beachfront Park.

To reach the Amelia Island State Park trailhead from I-95, follow the directions above to Amelia Island Pkwy. Turn right onto Amelia Island Pkwy., and follow it 2.5 miles (you'll pass through one traffic circle after 1.5 miles). Turn right onto Buccaneer Trail, and continue 1.2 miles to FL A1A S. Continue straight on FL A1A S. 4.9 miles through four traffic circles. Turn left into Amelia Island State Park. You'll find parking just beyond the entrance station. (Note that there is a small fee to park.)

Surrounded by coconut palms and meandering along the back of South Beach, the Atlantic Greenway (a segment of the nearly 3,000-mile East Coast Greenway system) is nestled in one of the United States' most popular destinations. Both of the trail's endpoints are located in calm areas of Miami Beach, not far from the Atlantic Ocean. As it draws closer to central South Beach, with its popular bars and hotels, it starts to bustle with foot traffic.

There are large, grassy areas with exercise spots and volleyball courts, people longboarding, street artists, and plenty of people using the trail for access to the wonderfully bathtub-like Miami ocean water.

The southern endpoint starts at South Pointe Beach and Pier—Miami Beach's southernmost tip—where you can walk out over the water and take in beautiful views of the Atlantic. Just behind the pier is an artfully laid-out

The East Coast Greenway meanders through one of the United States' most popular destinations.

Location
Miami-Dade

Endpoints
South Pointe Pier at
3 Washington Ave. to
Indian Beach Park at
4601 Collins Ave.
(Miami Beach)

Mileage
4.2

Type
Greenway/Non-Rail-Trail

Roughness Index
1

Surfaces
Asphalt, Boardwalk,
Cement

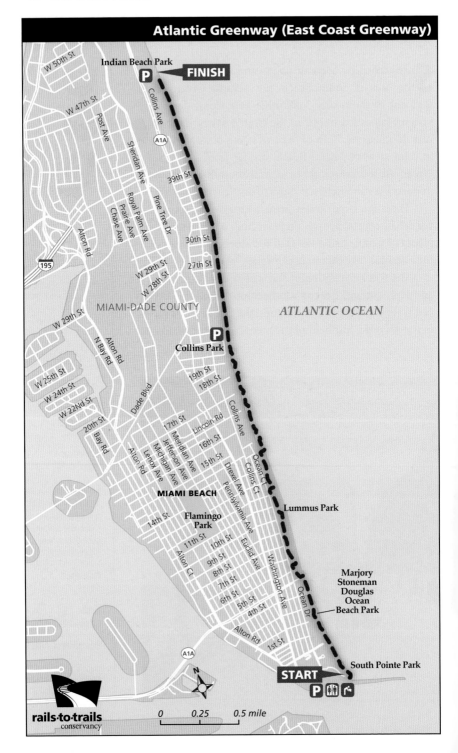

Atlantic Greenway (East Coast Greenway)

Indian Beach Park

FINISH

W 50th St
W 47th St
Post Ave
Sheridan Ave
Royal Palm Ave
Prairie Ave
Chase Ave
Pine Tree Dr
Alton Rd
Collins Ave
A1A
39th St
30th St
27th St
W 29th St
W 28th St
195

MIAMI-DADE COUNTY

ATLANTIC OCEAN

Collins Park

W 29th St
N Bay Rd
Alton Rd
Dade Blvd
19th St
18th St
Collins Ave
W 25th St
W 24th St
W 22nd St
20th St
Bay Rd
Alton Rd
17th St
Meridian Ave
Jefferson Ave
Michigan Ave
Lenox Ave
Lincoln Rd
16th St
15th St
Drexel Ave
Pennsylvania Ave
Collins Ct
Ocean Ct
Washington Ave

MIAMI BEACH

Flamingo Park

14th St
11th St
10th St
9th St
8th St
7th St
6th St
5th St
4th St
Alton Ct
Euclid Ave
Ocean Dr
Alton Rd
1st St

Lummus Park

Marjory
Stoneman
Douglas
Ocean
Beach Park

A1A

N

START

South Pointe Park

rails·to·trails
conservancy

0   0.25   0.5 mile

small park, with a winding trail and a small ice cream shop in the middle. Heading north, the smooth, red-orange-patterned concrete trail becomes increasingly dotted on the left with shops, hotels, bars, and restaurants. Interesting sculptures, rocks, and places to stop and rest pepper the length of the trail. You'll also pass frequent water stations for washing off beach sand, as well as several public restrooms.

Past the busy stretch of Central South Beach, large segments of the trail turn into what is known as the Miami Beach Boardwalk, where bike riding is prohibited. Along the way, behind a series of buildings, are a few unfinished segments of trail; however, these segments quickly give way to paved pathway.

The boardwalk ends just above Mid-Beach, and the trail continues with its smooth, pattern-painted concrete for about a quarter mile before it ends at a small roundabout at Indian Beach Park (a sign labels this gem as EAST COAST GREENWAY).

CONTACT: tinyurl.com/atlgreenway

DIRECTIONS

To reach the South Pointe Pier trailhead from I-95 S., take Exit 2D toward I-395 E./Miami Beach (0.9 mile), which merges into FL A1A/MacArthur Causeway (0.4 mile). Continue on FL A1A 3.6 miles to Miami Beach; it turns into Fifth St. for about six blocks. Turn right onto Washington Ave., and continue 0.5 mile to Inlet Blvd. Turn left onto Inlet Blvd. Parking is available along the street and at the South Pointe Park and Pier, as well as at the end of the road and where the trail starts.

To reach the Indian Beach trailhead from I-95, take Exit 4 to merge onto I-195 E., and continue 4.7 miles, crossing the bridge to Miami Beach. Continue on W. 41st St. 0.7 mile, and turn left onto Indian Creek Drive/Collins Ave. Follow Indian Creek Drive about 0.3 mile to the start of the trail on your right at Indian Beach Park (along the back of the beach). There is a large parking lot in front of the park along the road.

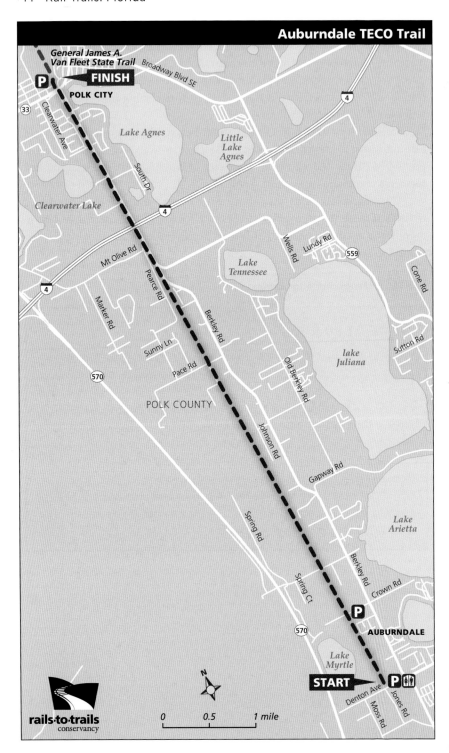

Auburndale TECO Trail

The Auburndale TECO Trail connects Lake Myrtle in Auburndale with Polk City, where it meets up with the General James A. Van Fleet Trail. The flat route and smooth surface are inviting to users of all types and skills.

The trailhead at the southern end of the trail on Denton Avenue in Auburndale is a good place to start. Here, you will find plenty of parking, drinking water, and public restrooms. Views to the west over farms and wild meadows from the parking lot will prepare you for the bucolic inland Florida landscapes that await you.

A few hundred meters north of Denton Avenue, you'll reach the Auburndale City Dog Park, a popular destination for four-legged trail users and their bipedal friends. Heading farther north, the former railroad grade passes through two lakes situated on either side of the trail before reaching the impressive Lake Myrtle Sports

The flat route and smooth surface of the Auburndale TECO is inviting to all types and skills of trail users.

Location
Polk

Endpoints
318 Denton Ave.
(Auburndale) to
Berkley Road and
FL 33 (Polk City)

Mileage
6.6

Type
Rail-Trail

Roughness Index
1

Surface
Asphalt, Concrete

Complex. The complex reminds trail users that even though the surrounding area is reminiscent of rustic swamp and scrubland, the trail is never that far from residential communities.

Proceeding farther north, the trail is collocated with an overhead utility line, eventually taking on a more rustic feel as it continues to Polk City. Along the way, you'll pass through forests of southern pine and oak offering occasional shade, with sassafras and wildflower patches in sunny spots. The trail weaves in and out of wetland marshes and swamps and then passes through cattle farms with scenic tree stands and the occasional barn and farmhouse.

Arriving at the northern terminus, you have the option to head farther north on the Van Fleet Trail or return to the Denton Avenue trailhead. Keep an eye out for bald eagles, herons, and more as the flat expanses offer wide-open vistas to take in the picturesque farmland and rural feel of inland central Florida.

CONTACT: auburndalefl.com/parks

DIRECTIONS

To reach the southern trailhead at Denton Ave. from I-4, take Exit 44 for FL 559 toward Polk City/Auburndale (0.3 mile). Head south on FL 559 for 0.9 mile, and then turn right onto County Road 559A. Continue 1.9 miles, and turn left onto Berkley Road. Continue 4.7 miles to the intersection with Denton Ave., and turn right at the light. The trailhead is on the right at 318 Denton Ave. (Parking is available for people with disabilities.)

To reach the trail's northern end at FL 33 from I-4, take Exit 44 for FL 559 toward Polk City/Auburndale (0.3 mile), and head north on FL 559 N. Continue 0.6 mile, and turn left to stay on FL 559 N. After 1.8 miles, turn left onto Commonwealth Ave. N./FL 33. In 0.2 mile turn right onto Berkley Road. Almost immediately, before the road curves south, you will see the trailhead and parking area in a small park just north of Berkley Road. Although there is an information kiosk and a playground, there are no amenities such as restrooms and drinking water at the northern end. (Parking is available for people with disabilities.)

The Black Creek Trail connects Black Point Park and Marina in Homestead to Larry and Penny Thompson Park in Miami. At Black Point Park, you can enter Biscayne National Park via a short, quarter-mile gravel trail that leads directly to the Atlantic Ocean. Thin-tire bikes need to be walked through this gravel section, which is well worth the effort for the open-water views of Biscayne Bay. The public marina also has restrooms and a restaurant; be sure to bring a bike lock as bikes are not permitted inside the deck area. The restaurant also provides good views of the water, where manatees and alligators coexist.

Begin your journey in the park, and follow signs that mark the trail. There is also a signed connection to the Biscayne Trail, which heads north and then connects with the Old Cutler Trail. Continuing from Black Point Park and Marina, the trail heads northwest and mostly

The Black Creek Trail follows alongside a canal for most of the pathway's length.

Location
Miami-Dade

Endpoints
Black Point Park and Marina near S.W. 87th Ave. and S.W. 248th St. (Homestead) to S.W. 176th St. and Lindgren Road, near Larry and Penny Thompson Park (Miami)

Mileage
8.5

Type
Greenway/Non-Rail-Trail

Roughness Index
1

Surface
Asphalt, Concrete, Gravel

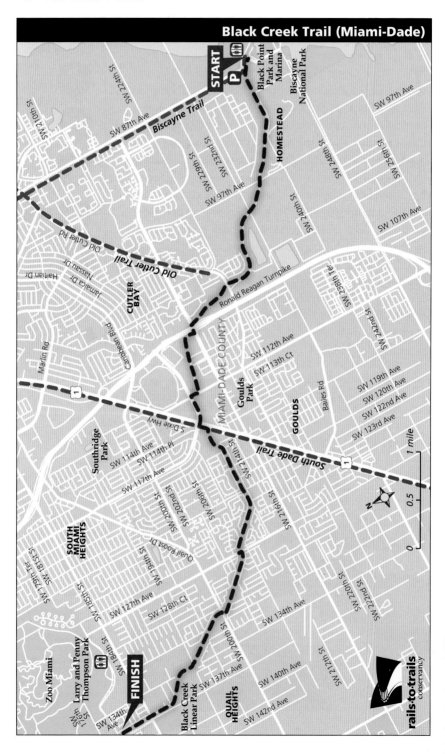

Black Creek Trail (Miami-Dade)

follows a canal bank. Expect to see iguanas scurrying into the water, as well as a variety of birds. The trail passes through various public works facilities and alongside neighborhoods.

While the trail has a rural feel, there are commercial establishments nearby, as well as the South Miami-Dade Cultural Arts Center, located where the trail intersects US 1/South Dixie Highway. From here, the trail connects to the South Dade Trail, which follows the dedicated MetroBus service. Bicycles are permitted on the bus system as well as on the connecting MetroRail service to the north. East of US 1, the trail has a direct and marked connection with the Old Cutler Trail.

The trail ends slightly farther west of Larry and Penny Thompson Park, which has public restrooms, camping, and a seasonal water park. Adjacent to the park off Southwest 152nd Street are the Gold Coast Railroad Museum, where you can ride a locomotive and learn about Florida's railroad history, and Zoo Miami, Florida's oldest zoo, with more than 200 different animals under its care. Note that there is no direct off-road connection from the trail to these sites.

CONTACT: www.miamidade.gov/parksmasterplan/library/blackcreektrail.pdf

DIRECTIONS

From Miami: To reach the Homestead trailhead at Black Point Park and Marina (24775 S.W. 87th Ave.) from I-75 S., take Exit 5 for Florida's Turnpike. Merge onto Ronald Reagan Turnpike (toll road), and go 26.6 miles. Take Exit 11 for Cutler Ridge Blvd. toward S.W. 216th St. Continue straight on S.W. 108th Court, and in 0.4 mile, turn left onto S.W. 216th St. Turn right onto S.W. 07th Ave. Continue 1.5 miles. Turn right to enter the park (which remains S.W. 87th Ave.); follow the road about 0.1 mile into the marina. Look for parking on your left by the docks. Parking is also located past the park entrance to your right along S.W. 87th Ave.

To reach the northern trailhead at S.W. 176th St. and Lindgren Road from I-75 S., take Exit 5 for Florida's Turnpike. Merge onto Ronald Reagan Turnpike (toll road), and go 24.7 miles. Take Exit 13 for FL 994/Eureka Drive toward Quail Roost Drive. Turn right onto S.W. 184th St./ Eureka Drive, and follow it 2.3 miles. Turn right onto Lindgren Road. The trailhead will be in 0.5 mile to your right. You can enter Larry and Penny Thompson Park (12451 S.W. 184th St.) by turning right onto S.W. 176th St., which turns into Talbot Road (veering right); go 0.4 mile to the park entrance.

The trail is wheelchair accessible; marked parking for people with disabilities is available at Black Point Park and Marina for permit holders visiting the restaurant as well as at Larry and Penny Thompson Park.

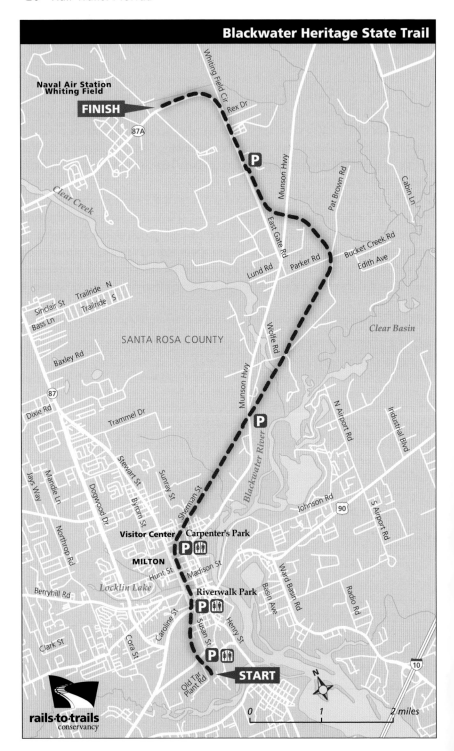

Blackwater Heritage State Trail

In Milton, just northeast of Pensacola, the nearly 10-mile Blackwater Heritage State Trail is the rewarding result of a partnership between Florida's Departments of Transportation and Environmental Protection, and the U.S. Navy. Five convenient trailheads provide access, while a smooth, asphalt surface promises an enjoyable ride through flat rural and urban areas.

The route follows the old Florida and Alabama Railroad, once operated by the Bagdad Land and Lumber Company to ship milled lumber from Bagdad to Whitley, Alabama. The railroad stopped running in 1939, but when America entered World War II, the rails were rebuilt and used to ship aviation fuel to Naval Air Station Whiting Field. The trail's northernmost 1.5 miles are officially dubbed the Military Heritage Trail.

Expect a more rural experience as you head north on the Blackwater Heritage State Trail.

Location
Santa Rosa

Endpoints
Old Tar Plant Road near Old US 90 to Naval Air Station Whiting Field entrance gate near E. Gate Road and Whiting Field Circle (Milton)

Mileage
9.6

Type
Rail-Trail

Roughness Index
1

Surface
Asphalt

Start at the southern trailhead on Old Tar Plant Road in Milton. The trailhead offers parking and restrooms, nearby restaurants, and a bicycle shop for last-minute gear and supplies. After 1 mile, you'll reach a visitor center (across the street from Milton Public Library) staffed by local residents, who provide information about the trail and other area parks and attractions. As the route streaks north, the surroundings become increasingly rural. Telltale signs that you're leaving Milton behind include trailside pitcher plants and rabbit sightings. By the time you reach the Munson Highway parking area, just under 3 miles into your journey, the rural setting dominates. Munson provides the only horse trailer parking, so expect to spot more equestrians on the adjacent trail and at the seven nearby shared stream crossings.

The trail ends abruptly at the gates of Naval Air Station Whiting Field. Before September 2001, the trail continued west to an active airport runway, but national and local security precautions now prevent access.

Shutterbugs take note: While the local military personnel embrace the trail, security officers at the base entrance may forbid individuals from taking pictures of the site.

CONTACT: floridastateparks.org/trail/blackwater

DIRECTIONS

To reach the southern trailhead at Old Tar Plant Road from I-10, take Exit 26 toward Milton/Bagdad (0.2 mile), and head north 3.1 miles on County Road 191/Garcon Point Road (signs for Bagdad/Milton). Turn left onto Taylor St. In 0.3 mile turn right onto Patterson Town Road, and then make a sharp left onto Old Tar Plant Road. Limited parking is available immediately to your left. The trail actually extends just slightly farther south.

To reach the Munson Hwy. parking area and its equestrian parking from I-10, take Exit 31 for FL 87 toward Milton/Navarre. Head north on FL 87, and go 1.2 miles. Turn left onto US 90. In 4.6 miles turn right onto Stewart St. In 0.8 mile turn right onto CR 191, and go 5 miles to the trail intersection.

To reach the Whiting Field trailhead from I-10, take Exit 31 for FL 87 toward Milton/Navarre. Head north on FL 87, and go 1.2 miles. Turn left onto US 90. In 4.6 miles turn right onto Stewart St. In 0.8 mile turn right onto CR 191, and continue a little more than 4.3 miles. Make a slight left onto E. Gate Road, and continue 1.3 miles. Trailhead parking will be on your right.

Once owned by Rails-to-Trails Conservancy, the Blountstown Greenway Bike Path inhabits a portion of the Marianna & Blountstown (M&B) Railroad, which connected the Apalachicola River town of Blountstown with the Chipola River town of Marianna. The rail-trail is also a designated part of the Florida National Scenic Trail, a hiking and backpacking route that stretches more than 1,000 miles from the Georgia border to the Everglades.

Operating between 1909 and 1972, the M&B Railroad, nicknamed affectionately by locals as both "Meat and Bread" and "Many Bumps," was an important source of transportation and shipping for Calhoun County, hauling passengers, mail, lumber, agricultural products, building products, and manufacturing goods. The trail project includes a restored railroad depot, now part of M&B Railroad Memorial Park, where an original steam locomotive (number 444) and its red caboose are located.

The short Blountstown Greenway Bike Path is part of the 1,000-mile Florida National Scenic Trail.

Location
Calhoun

Endpoints
Sam Atkins Park at N.W. Silas Green St. and 16th St. to Neal Landing Public Boat Ramp at S.E. River St. and Apalachicola River (Blountstown)

Mileage
3.4

Type
Rail-Trail

Roughness Index
1

Surface
Asphalt, Concrete

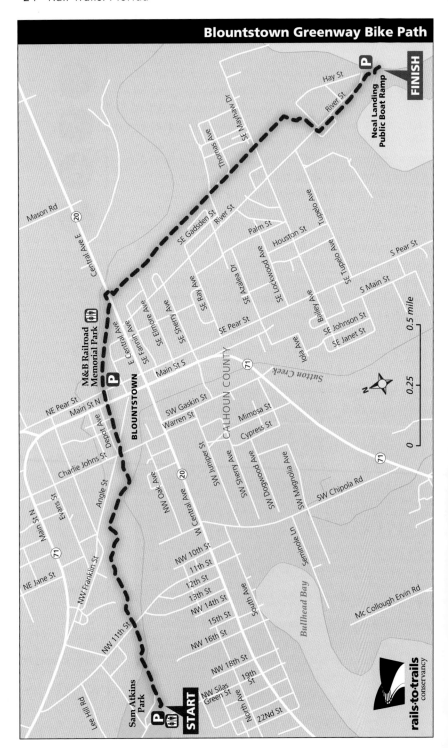

Start at the northern endpoint at Sam Atkins Park, which has ample parking and restrooms. You'll head south toward the Apalachicola River, passing through the heart of charming Blountstown. The town is named after Creek Indian Chief Blount, and Indian artifacts are displayed at Panhandle Pioneer Settlement, just north of Sam Atkins Park. With several historical buildings—including a schoolhouse, a blacksmith shop, a gristmill, and others—in a rustic farm setting, the museum complex provides a glimpse of life in northwest Florida during the 19th and early 20th centuries.

As the route ventures south, pine forest canopies and gently rolling hills give way to swampy lowlands. About midway through your journey, you'll reach M&B Railroad Memorial Park, located between Main Street and North Pear Street (public parking is available one block south and to the left). The complex includes a train-themed playground, a covered picnic area, and restrooms. Several locally owned restaurants are within walking distance.

The trail then conveniently passes underneath busy FL 20, eventually reaching the trail's southeast terminus at Neal Landing Public Boat Ramp on the Apalachicola River. Through a local program to encourage safe swimming for kids, life vests are available for children who choose to take a dip in the river with their supervising adult.

CONTACT: calhouncountyfl.org/community.html

DIRECTIONS

To reach the Sam Atkins Park trailhead from I-10, take Exit 142 for FL 71 toward Marianna/Blountstown (0.4 mile). Head south on FL 71 S. (signs for Altha/Blountstown), and continue 20.4 miles. Turn right onto 11th St., go 1 mile, and turn right onto FL 20 W. After 0.5 mile, turn right onto 19th St. After about 0.3 mile, you'll reach the park. Turn right into the parking lot, which is adjacent to the trail entrance. Another parking lot is located past the trailhead parking lot, to your left.

To reach the southern trailhead at Neal Landing Public Boat Ramp from I-10, take Exit 152 for FL 69 toward Grand Ridge/Blountstown (0.4 mile), and head south on FL 69 for 14.9 miles. Turn left onto Main St. N., and continue 0.5 mile. Turn left onto Central Ave. E., go 0.3 mile, and then turn right onto S.E. River St. After 1.4 miles, turn right into the trailhead.

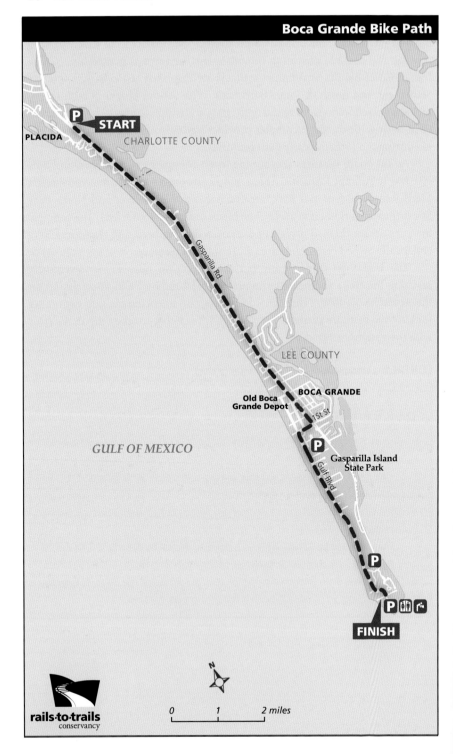

Boca Grande Bike Path

PLACIDA

START

CHARLOTTE COUNTY

Gasparilla Rd

LEE COUNTY

Old Boca
Grande Depot

BOCA GRANDE

1st St

GULF OF MEXICO

Gasparilla Island
State Park

Gulf Blvd

FINISH

rails·to·trails
conservancy

N

0   1   2 miles

Visitors come to Gasparilla Island for its soothing beaches, upscale eateries, shopping, and the history in and around Boca Grande. You, too, can sample these amenities up and down this paved 6-mile trail, known locally as the Boca Grande Bike Path. Credited as Florida's first rail-trail, the path travels the length of the Gulf Coast barrier island, offering a host of activities from sunbathing to state park rambles.

Those who start from the north will have their pick of beautiful overlooks of Gasparilla Sound. Also watch for the iguanas (nonnative) that have successfully inhabited this lush, palm-covered island, as well as gopher tortoises. This end offers a separate jogging track. If you start from the south shore, be sure to stop at the Port Boca Grande Lighthouse, which dates back to 1890 and is the centerpiece of Gasparilla Island State Park. Visit the museum

The Boca Grande Bike Path has a dual track to accommodate both bikers and runners.

Location
Charlotte, Lee

Endpoints
Gasparilla Road near
Gulf Shores Drive
(Placida) to Gulf Blvd.
and Belcher Road
(Boca Grande)

Mileage
6

Type
Rail-Trail

Roughness Index
1

Surface
Asphalt

inside to learn about the island's history, or enjoy swimming, snorkeling, and fishing from the surrounding beaches.

Whichever direction you choose, the beautifully landscaped and well-kept trail soon reaches central Boca Grande, just south of the trail midpoint. The old Boca Grande Depot has been converted into an upscale commercial center, and a section of preserved track lies behind it. Surprisingly, golf carts harmoniously share the trail with other users, showcasing a unique blend of Southern hospitality and practical transportation for residents and visitors.

After exploring the Boca Grande Bike Path, check out the nearby 8-mile Cape Haze Pioneer Trail, north of Gasparilla Island. The two rail-trails follow the former Charlotte Harbor and Northern Railroad, which once serviced the state's early phosphate industry.

CONTACT: floridastateparks.org/park/Gasparilla-Island

DIRECTIONS

To access the northern trailhead from I-75, take Exit 193 for Jacaranda Blvd. toward Englewood/Venice/Sarasota County. Head south on Jacaranda Blvd., and go 5.1 miles. Turn left onto FL 776, and go 8.7 miles. Turn right onto Placida Road, and in 8.9 miles turn right onto the Boca Grande Causeway (toll required), which takes you to the island. In 1.9 miles you arrive on the island, and in another 0.5 mile the trailhead will be on the left.

Gasparilla Island State Park is accessible by following the above directions to Boca Grande Causeway (toll required), which takes you to the island. Go 6.3 miles on Boca Grande Causeway/FL 771/Gasparilla Road/Park Ave., and turn right onto First St. W. in downtown Boca Grande. Make a quick left onto Gulf Blvd., and drive 2 miles. The parking lot entrance is located immediately after Belcher Road. Restrooms and drinking water are also available in the state park. A small fee is required to park. Note: Another parking lot is available to the right (if you're traveling south on Gulf Blvd.) before you pass South Harbor Drive.

The 6.5-mile Cady Way Trail runs through a pleasant, lake-dotted route that links quaint neighborhoods, shopping areas, parks, and business districts between Winter Park and Orlando. Because of its location, many residents find the trail a convenient commuter and exercise route. The trail also provides several mirrors at blind corners and bridges over busy road crossings, making it a safer route for bicyclists and pedestrians.

The southern terminus of the trail at Herndon Avenue in Orlando, adjacent to Fashion Square Mall, is a good place to start your journey. Nearby, a small park named after the trail offers water, sheltered benches, and a full bike mount complete with tools to tune your bike.

Trail users on the Cady are treated to a pleasant, scenic route linking neighborhoods, parks, and businesses between Winter Park and Orlando.

Location
Orange

Endpoints
Fashion Square Mall/
Herndon Ave. (Orlando)
to Aloma Ave. and
Howell Branch Road/Hall
Road (Winter Park)

Mileage
6.5

Type
Rail-Trail

Roughness Index
1

Surface
Asphalt

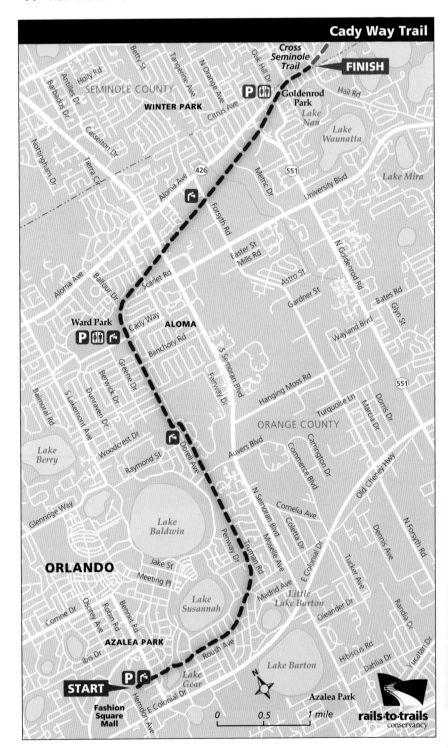

Surrounded by small lakes, the trail heads east briefly, curves left (north), and then continues straight through several neighborhoods and small parks and past a couple of schools.

At Cady Way, the trail veers right. Be sure to check out Ward Park on your left, which has several baseball diamonds and sports fields, a track, and a seasonal swimming pool. Heading northeast through the town of Aloma, you'll find yourself on the quiet back side of multiple businesses. The trail then opens up to a busier area, eventually terminating at the corner of Aloma Avenue and Howell Branch Road.

Near the endpoint of the Cady Way Trail, you'll find the southwestern terminus of the Cross Seminole Trail, which extends another 22.8 miles to Lake Mary.

CONTACT: orangecountyfl.net/CultureParks

DIRECTIONS

To reach the southern trailhead, from I-4 E., take Exit 83A for FL 50. Merge onto N. Garland Ave., and in 0.2 mile turn right onto Colonial Drive/FL 50. In 2.7 miles turn left onto Herndon Ave. The trailhead is 0.2 mile north, adjacent to Fashion Square Mall and a post office. From I-4 W., take Exit 84 and turn left onto Colonial Drive/FL 50. Follow the rest of the directions above.

To reach the Cady Way Park trailhead, take I-4 to Exit 87. Head east on W. Fairbanks Ave./FL 426, and go 3.6 miles. Turn right onto N. Lakemont Ave., and go 0.5 mile. Turn left onto Loch Berry Road, and in 0.2 mile turn left onto Perth Lane. Immediately turn right onto Cady Way. The park is 0.4 mile ahead on the left.

Goldenrod Park is another access point. From I-4, take Exit 87, and head east on W. Fairbanks Ave./FL 426; go 6.4 miles. Turn right onto N. Goldenrod Road, and the park is immediately on the left.

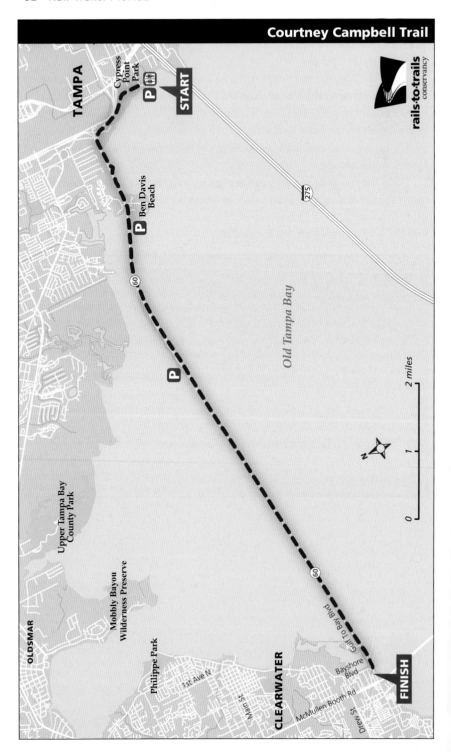

The Courtney Campbell Trail gives riders an experience uniquely Floridian, connecting Tampa to Clearwater across a portion of Old Tampa Bay. The trail starts inconspicuously near Cypress Point Park in Tampa. The first section of trail is highlighted by close-flying airliners as you skirt the west side of Tampa International Airport. The trail closely hugs the highway, the world headquarters of the Shriners, and a large hotel complex before finally opening up to views of Tampa Bay proper. Here, the trail is finally next to its namesake, the Courtney Campbell Causeway. Ben Davis Beach, a major trailhead, parking area, and landmark, emerges on the south side of the trail. A bike fix-it station equipped with tools and an air pump is conveniently located here.

The 9 miles of causeway trail highlight unfettered views of the bay punctuated by informative interpretive

The Courtney Campbell Trail delivers a uniquely Floridian experience across a portion of Old Tampa Bay.

Location
Hillsborough, Pinellas

Endpoints
Cypress Point Park at W. Cypress St. near FL 589 (Tampa) to FL 60/Gulf to Bay Blvd. and S. Bayshore Blvd. (Clearwater)

Mileage
10.5

Type
Greenway/Non-Rail-Trail

Roughness Index
1

Surface
Asphalt, Concrete

signage explaining the historical and natural resources you are likely to encounter. The trail caters to animal lovers; keep an eye out for marine wildlife, including dolphins, as well as a plethora of bird species.

Upon exiting land and continuing on the bridge of the causeway, trail users encounter a fabulous structure. The causeway trail bridge is completely separated from the highway itself and extends for 0.75 mile. The observation platforms near the top of this bridge provide great photo opportunities and views. There are multiple trailheads along the causeway for those wishing to make a shorter visit. Fishing boats, personal watercraft, and recreational boats are constants on the water along the trail and make for interesting scenery. The trail ends just after reaching Clearwater at Gulf to Bay Boulevard and Bayshore Boulevard.

CONTACT: courtneycampbell.org

DIRECTIONS

To reach the eastern trailhead at Cypress Point Park from I-275 S., take Exit 39 for FL 60 W. toward FL 589 N./Clearwater/Tampa International Airport, and almost immediately exit at Spruce St. Head east on W. Spruce St., and then immediately turn right onto N. O'Brien St. In 0.5 mile turn right onto W. Cypress St. In 0.6 mile turn left into Bay West Commerce Park; this dead-ends into the park.

To reach the trailhead at Ben T. Davis Park from I-275, take Exit 39 for FL 60 W. toward FL 589 N./Clearwater/Tampa International Airport. In 1.7 miles, take Exit 2A for FL 60 W. Continue on FL 60 W. 1.5 miles, and turn left. Ben T. Davis Park is on the south side of the road.

Stretching from Orlando's densely populated outskirts to the sleepy bedroom communities of Oviedo, Winter Springs, and Lake Mary, the Cross Seminole Trail provides crucial residential links in an automobile-dominated region. The trail comprises three separate sections that will eventually connect to create an impressive 23-mile continuous trail. Along the way, you'll pass through diverse settings, including urban roadways, hammock preserves, and parkland. Currently, the gaps between the sections are not well marked, so use caution at these points.

The open sections total some 22 miles and connect to other area rail-trails: the 14-mile Seminole Wekiva Trail to the west and the 6-mile Cady Way Trail to the south.

The 6.4-mile southern section starts on the northeast corner of the Aloma Avenue/Howell Branch Road intersection on the Seminole–Orange county line. (Signs for

The Cross Seminole Trail provides crucial connections for bikers and walkers in an automobile-dominated region.

Location
Seminole

Endpoints
Howell Branch Road and Aloma Ave./FL 426 (Aloma) to H. E. Thomas Jr. Pkwy. and Rinehart Road (Lake Mary)

Mileage
22.8

Type
Rail-Trail

Roughness Index
1

Surface
Asphalt

Cross Seminole Trail

rails-to-trails
conservancy

the Cady Way Trail mark the opposite corner.) Note that there is no formal parking at this endpoint; the best place to find parking on the eastern side of the Cross Seminole Trail is at the Black Hammock trailhead in Winter Springs.

This section follows Aloma Avenue northeast though a largely urban setting, ending at Central Avenue in Oviedo, four blocks from the start of the second section. Rather than crossing South Central Avenue, turn left onto the western side street; the trail picks up just north of CrossLife Church Legacy Hall. (Currently, a small section of trail continues across South Central Avenue and ends abruptly at Oviedo Boulevard with inadequate signage to the next section.)

The second section extends northwest from downtown Oviedo to Winter Springs. From the intersection of Railroad Street and North Central Avenue, you'll enter a pleasant wooded area and wind through several quiet, upscale neighborhoods. After 3.5 miles, you'll reach the Black Hammock trailhead, which offers the only sufficient parking along this section. There is a beautifully constructed concrete pedestrian bridge with a padded equestrian path that crosses FL 434. From there, the trail passes Winter Springs High School and Central Winds Park, Seminole County's premier public park, as it threads through peaceful neighborhoods. Just after passing over the Gee Creek Bridge, you'll reach the endpoint of this trail segment at Layer Elementary School. Take a left, and then turn right onto the shoulder bike lane of FL 419. Make a right onto Wade Street. This area is highly industrial with heavy machinery and truck traffic; use caution. Turn left onto Old Sanford Oviedo Road. The road ends at a recycling center with a gravel/wood-chip road continuing on the right side near a guardrail. This small roadway will lead to the start of the third segment of the trail.

The third section begins along 3 miles of a utility throughway and through Soldier's Creek Park. The trail crosses US 17/92 via a nice overpass and ends at Big Tree Park in historic Longwood. Here you can see the remnants of "The Senator," a large pond cypress that was once the biggest and oldest of its kind in the world until it burned down in 2012. Nearby stands Lady Liberty, a nearly 2,000-year-old cypress standing almost 90 feet tall.

At North Ronald Reagan Boulevard, you'll head left a short distance and then immediately turn right (north) onto a sidewalk trail section along Longwood Lake Mary Road. You'll travel briefly through a suburban residential area, after which the trail cuts left and runs along the right side of Green Way Boulevard. Immediately after turning, you'll pass Greenwood Lakes Park, a small residential open space with a playground, library, and fitness stations along the trail. The trail then turns right shortly before reaching Queensbridge Drive.

The final 4 miles of the trail differ from the previous sections. The largely urban path parallels busy Rinehart Road in Lake Mary for much of its length.

Take the trail to its end at FL 46A and H. E. Thomas Jr. Parkway, and you'll follow a bustling business corridor with many road crossings. Several fitness stations are located along this section of trail. If you need a break from high-volume traffic once you reach trail's end, simply hop on the connecting spur to the Seminole Wekiva Trail on the west side of Rinehart Road at the Oakland Hills Circle intersection.

CONTACT: seminolecountyfl.gov

DIRECTIONS

To Section 1 (Goldenrod Park): From I-4, take Exit 87, and head east on W. Fairbanks Ave./FL 426; go 6.4 miles. Turn right onto N. Goldenrod Road, and the park is immediately on the left.

To Section 2 (Black Hammock trailhead): From downtown Orlando, take I-4 to Exit 94 for FL 434 toward Longwood/Winter Springs. Head northeast on FL 434, and go 10.2 miles. Turn right onto Jetta Point and into the well-marked parking lot.

To Section 3 (Layer Elementary School): From downtown Orlando, take I-4 to Exit 94 for FL 434 toward Longwood/Winter Springs. Head northeast on FL 434, and go 6.1 miles. Turn left onto FL 419, and in 0.2 mile take a right into Layer Elementary School. The trail will be on your right.

To Section 4 (Lake Mary trailhead): From downtown Orlando, take I-4 to Exit 98 toward Lake Mary/Heathrow. Head east on Lake Mary Blvd. 1 mile; the trailhead is on the northeast corner of Lake Mary Blvd. and Rinehart Road.

The East Central Regional Rail Trail follows a set of railroad tracks built in 1885 to transport cargo and passengers from the Atlantic Coast into central Florida. Totaling about 15 miles at the time of publication, the trail will eventually stretch more than 50 miles from DeBary to Edgewater, with another segment to Titusville, making it one of the longest rail-trail conversions in the state.

Providence Blvd. and Perimeter Drive (Deltona) to Corral Road/Guise Road near Osteen-Maytown Road (Osteen): 13 miles

The westernmost segment of the trail starts at Providence Boulevard and Perimeter Drive in Deltona, which is also the location for the eastern terminus of the Spring to Spring Trail (see page 140). Heading east, you'll soon reach Green Springs Park (to your right), one of only a few

Location
Brevard, Volusia

Endpoints
Providence Blvd. and Perimeter Drive (Deltona) to Corral Road/Guise Road near Osteen-Maytown Road (Osteen); W. Park Ave. and Dale Ave. to Cow Creek Road south of Eels Grove Road (Edgewater); LaGrange Road and US 1 to Draa Road and Norwood Ave. (Titusville)

Mileage
15

Type
Rail-Trail

Roughness Index
1

Surface
Asphalt, Concrete

When complete, the East Central Regional Rail Trail will stretch more than 50 miles.

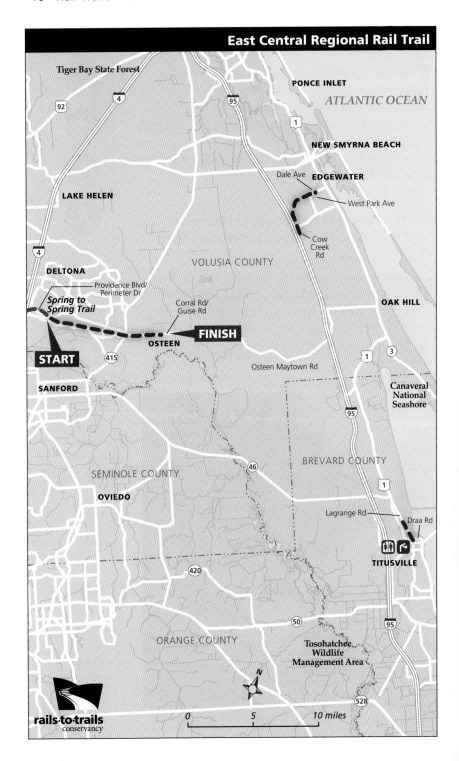

East Central Regional Rail Trail

Tiger Bay State Forest

PONCE INLET

ATLANTIC OCEAN

92

4

95

1

NEW SMYRNA BEACH

Dale Ave EDGEWATER

LAKE HELEN

West Park Ave

4

Cow
Creek
Rd

VOLUSIA COUNTY

DELTONA

Providence Blvd/
Perimeter Dr

OAK HILL

*Spring to
Spring Trail*

Corral Rd/
Guise Rd

FINISH

START

415

OSTEEN

1

3

SANFORD

Osteen Maytown Rd

1

Canaveral
National
Seashore

95

BREVARD COUNTY

SEMINOLE COUNTY

46

OVIEDO

1

Lagrange Rd

Draa Rd

TITUSVILLE

420

ORANGE COUNTY

50

95

Tosohatchee
Wildlife
Management Area

N

rails·to·trails
conservancy

0   5   10 miles

528

remaining green sulfur springs in Florida. Here, you'll find natural trails, scenic overlooks, a playground, and picnic pavilions. This segment of trail also provides a canopy of oak trees that provides cool shade from the strong Florida sun.

Making your way to the middle of the trail segment, you'll start to pass informational kiosks with information about the corridor's railroad past and eventual transformation into a rail-trail. Just northeast of Ledford Road to your left is Audubon Park, a storm-water management and natural resource preservation area that hosts almost 50 bird species.

Along the route, the high tree walls make you forget you're in a populated area. A long bridge transports you over FL 415, after which the trail passes through an open area for about 1 mile. Once past Deer Run Road, the trail makes an abrupt right and then quickly curves left, continuing into a heavily wooded area toward the eastern terminus at Corral Road (you can see railroad tracks extending into the woods). Wildlife is not as prominent here as it is on other Florida trails, but if you keep an eye out, you can spot sandhill cranes, kingfishers, and the occasional tortoise.

DIRECTIONS

Note that the western endpoint is located in a commercial area, and the eastern endpoint is located in a rural area—neither of which provide formal trail parking. A wide shoulder along the eastern end of the trail does provide room for informal parking.

To reach the western endpoint at Providence Blvd. from I-4, take Exit 108 toward Deltona/DeBary. Turn left onto Debary Ave. After 2 miles, turn right onto Providence Blvd. After 0.1 mile, the trail endpoint will be on the left.

To reach the eastern endpoint at Guise Road, follow the directions above until you reach Debary Ave. Turn left onto Debary Ave., and in 2.2 miles continue straight on Doyle Road another 5.9 miles. Turn right onto FL 415, and in 0.2 mile turn left onto New Smyrna Blvd. Take the third left onto Florida Ave./Osteen-Maytown Road, and continue 2.6 miles. Turn right onto Guise Road; the trail endpoint will be on the left.

W. Park Ave. and Dale Ave. to Cow Creek Road south of Eels Grove Road (Edgewater): 0.5 mile

Opened in 2015, this short segment (approximately 0.5 mile) in Edgewater begins at the intersection of West Park Avenue and Dale Avenue and travels southwest through hammock habitat that parallels Park Avenue and Massey Road. The pathway turns south before reaching an impressive overpass crossing Indian River Boulevard.

DIRECTIONS

To reach the Cow Creek Road trailhead from I-95, take Exit 244 for FL 442 toward Edgewater/ Oak Hill, and head east on Indian River Blvd./FL 442. In 0.4 mile turn right onto Cow Creek Road, and look for parking to your left in 0.3 mile, just past Eels Grove Road. The trailhead is located another 0.2 mile ahead and to your right.

LaGrange Road and US 1 to Draa Road and Norwood Ave. (Titusville): 1.5 miles

A small suburban/commercial 1.5-mile segment of trail extends from LaGrange Road to Draa Road in Titusville. No formal trail parking is available for this section, which serves largely as a local community connector.

DIRECTIONS

To reach the northern endpoint from I-95, take Exit 223 for FL 46 toward Sanford/Miami. Head east on FL 46/W. Main St. 1.6 miles. Turn right onto US 1 S., and go 2.2 miles. Turn right onto LaGrange Road. The endpoint will be to your right.

CONTACT: volusia.org/services/community-services/parks-recreation-and-culture

El Rio Trail is a pleasant green corridor running along the east side of the El Rio Canal between Glades Road and Congress Avenue, just north of Northwest 82nd Boulevard. The trail offers several ways to experience the diversity of South Florida's natural environment. Many residents enjoy bass fishing in the canal, and plentiful egrets and great blue herons populate the corridor. Other birds, such as Muscovy ducks and ibis, are also common in the canal, and you may encounter iguanas as well.

Just off the trail are two unique options for exploring the native plants and landscape of the area: the Yamato Scrub Natural Area and Delray Oaks Natural Area. Yamato Scrub, located between Clint Moore Road and Congress Avenue, can be accessed directly from the trail. It includes more than 3 miles of trails that are primarily composed of natural surface; there is also a short paved trail. The Delray Oaks Natural Area is just north

This pleasant 4.7-mile corridor runs alongside the El Rio Canal, a popular local fishing hole.

Location
Palm Beach

Endpoints
Congress Ave. near N.W. 82nd Blvd. to Glades Road/FL 808 near N.W. 13th St. (Boca Raton)

Mileage
4.7

Type
Rail-Trail

Roughness Index
1

Surface
Asphalt

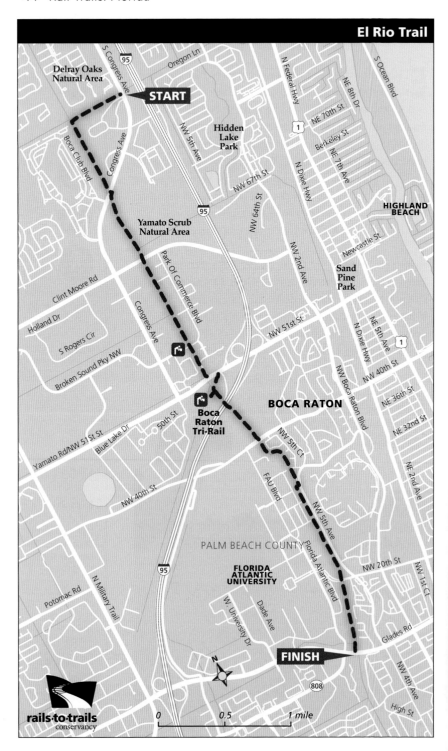

El Rio Trail

of the trail's terminus on Congress Avenue. Considerably smaller than Yamato Scrub, Delray Oaks also includes a short nature trail. Both natural areas feature several types of environments native to the area, including scrub, forested areas, and wetlands, and offer opportunities for wildlife viewing. Both areas also include bike racks.

Just south of Yamato Road, the trail provides a connection to the Boca Raton Tri-Rail station, which provides a convenient way to access the trail and includes bike lockers for those looking for a bike-to-transit option. Crossing Yamato Road is difficult and requires navigating six lanes of traffic and a CSX Railroad track crossing. An underpass is being built that will cross under Yamato Road and the tracks to connect the two pieces of trail. It is scheduled to be completed in late 2016. To reach a traffic signal to cross Yamato from the south, the most direct route is to cut through the Boca Village Plaza Shopping Center behind the Tri-Rail station, where Technology Way intersects with Yamato, and then follow the sidewalk east back to the trail.

CONTACT: myboca.us/pages/traffic/bicyclespedestrians-maps

DIRECTIONS

Parking near the trail is limited because of a lack of on-street spaces.

To reach the northern endpoint from I-95, take Exit 50 for Congress Ave. Head west on Peninsula Corp Drive, and immediately turn right onto Congress Ave. Drive 0.2 mile; the trailhead will be to your left just before the Gulf Stream. There is no formal trail parking at this endpoint.

To reach the south end of the El Rio Trail, take I-95 to Exit 45 for FL 808. Head east on FL 808/Glades Road 1.5 miles. The trail is just past the Florida Atlantic University campus, adjacent to the Gulf Stream canal. There is no formal trail parking at this endpoint.

Small parking lots are available at the Delray Oaks Natural Area off S.W. 29th St., just west of Congress Ave. near the north end of the trail, and at Yamato Scrub Natural Area on Clint Moore Road, 0.4 mile east of Congress Ave. From I-95, take Exit 50 for Congress Ave. Head west on Peninsula Corp Drive, and immediately turn right onto Congress Ave. Drive 0.4 mile, and turn left onto S.W. 29th St. Delray Oaks Natural Area is on the right. To reach the Yamato Scrub Natural Area, take I-95 to Exit 48 or 48A. Head east on FL 794/Yamato Road, and go 0.9 mile. Turn left onto N.W. Second Ave. In 0.5 mile turn left onto Jeffrey St. Continue straight 0.4 mile on Clint Moore Road, and the natural area will be on the right.

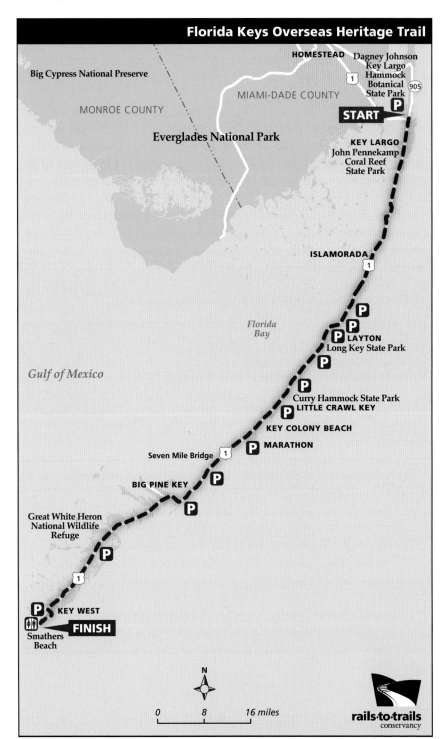

Florida Keys Overseas Heritage Trail

HOMESTEAD   Dagney Johnson
Key Largo
Big Cypress National Preserve   Hammock
Botanical   905
MIAMI-DADE COUNTY   State Park

START

MONROE COUNTY

Everglades National Park

KEY LARGO
John Pennekamp
Coral Reef
State Park

ISLAMORADA

Florida
Bay

LAYTON
Long Key State Park

Gulf of Mexico

Curry Hammock State Park
LITTLE CRAWL KEY

KEY COLONY BEACH

MARATHON
Seven Mile Bridge

BIG PINE KEY

Great White Heron
National Wildlife
Refuge

KEY WEST

FINISH

Smathers
Beach

N

0   8   16 miles

rails·to·trails
conservancy

When this former railroad corridor connecting Key West to the Florida mainland was originally operated by Henry Flagler as the Overseas Railroad in the early 1900s, many considered it the Eighth Wonder of the World. Today, the task of fully connecting dozens of islands into a first-class trail is a no-less-significant undertaking, with small man-made causeways and environmental issues creating challenges for trail builders.

At the time of publication, close to 80 miles of the 106.5-mile route have been completed, and various sections are under development or redevelopment. Additionally, many of the corridor's 23 railroad bridges are being repaired and, when complete, will greatly enhance connectivity.

When planning your trip, consider your skill level and comfort with roadways, and be sure to pack sunscreen and water. For a lower-stress experience, stay on the completed sections of trail on the northern half of the route to Marathon. If you wish to travel the entire route from Key Largo to Key West, be prepared for sections comprising busy roadways and bridges.

The Florida Keys Overseas Heritage Trail provides amazing ocean views of the 106.5-mile route between Key Largo and Key West.

Location
Monroe

Endpoints
County Road 905 and just north of Loquat Drive (Key Largo) to White Street Fishing Pier at White St. and Atlantic Blvd. (Key West)

Mileage
106.5 (about 80 completed)

Type
Rail-Trail

Roughness Index
1–2

Surface
Asphalt, Concrete

In addition to scenic ocean overlooks, there are numerous opportunities for activities along the trail, including kayaking through mangroves, visiting botanical gardens, hand-feeding tarpons, and enjoying the eclectic Keys lifestyle. Riding south from Key Largo, you'll pass 10 state parks, most of which are adjacent to the route. Notable parks include Dagny Johnson Key Largo Hammock Botanical State Park, John Pennekamp Coral Reef State Park in Key Largo, Long Key State Park, and Curry Hammock State Park in Little Crawl Key. Be sure to visit the Old Seven Mile Bridge near the trail's halfway point just after Marathon; it is listed on the National Register of Historic Places. A 3-mile section leading to Pigeon Key is still open to the public; there you'll find a museum documenting the construction of the Overseas Railroad. Work to rehabilitate the bridge is slated to begin in 2016.

Currently, the only way to reach the trail's southwest terminus at Key West is via the new Seven Mile Bridge, which crosses 7 miles of open water along FL A1A. The bridge contains a wide shoulder; however, be prepared for the sizable uphill climb to cross the bridge span, and be mindful of potential headwinds or crosswinds. As you approach Smathers Beach in Key West, you'll find beautiful views of the Atlantic Ocean, as well as parking, restrooms, showers, and a plethora of beach amenities. A right on Bertha Street and a left onto Atlantic Boulevard takes you to White Street. Turn left onto White Street to reach the trail's southern terminus at the White Street Fishing Pier.

CONTACT: floridastateparks.org/trail/Florida-Keys

DIRECTIONS

To reach the Key Largo trailhead from I-75 S., take Exit 5 for Florida's Turnpike. Merge onto Ronald Reagan Turnpike (toll road), and go 34.9 miles. Take Exit 1 onto US 1 S./N.E. First Ave. toward Key West, and go 21.7 miles (partial toll road). Turn left onto County Road 905. After 0.4 mile, turn right into the trailhead parking lot. (The lot is located just past Loquat Drive in Dagny Johnson Key Largo Hammock Botanical State Park.)

To reach the southern terminus in Key West, follow directions above to US 1 S. Take US 1 S. 124 miles (partial toll road). Turn left onto S. Roosevelt Blvd., and go 2.9 miles. Once you pass Seaside Drive on your right, look for parking along the street (to your left). S. Roosevelt Blvd. turns slightly right and becomes Bertha St. (Before Bertha St., look for street parking on your left.) After 0.2 mile, turn left onto Atlantic Blvd. Drive 0.5 mile, and turn left onto White St. You'll reach the terminus in 0.2 mile.

Parking and restrooms are located at all Florida State Parks (there is a fee to enter). The trail can also be accessed at numerous roadway intersections along the route.

Running between Lakeland and Bartow in suburban Polk County, the Fort Fraser Trail operates on a portion of the former South Florida Railroad's Pemberton Ferry Branch. Built in 1885, the line connected the present-day ghost town of Pemberton Ferry in the north with Bartow in the south, passing through the railroad's main line in Lakeland along the way. The sole stop between Lakeland and Bartow was in Highland City, now home to the Fort Fraser Trail's main trailhead.

In the north, the trail begins on the outskirts of Lakeland, not far from Polk State College. For the entire route, busy US 98 is within sight and earshot. However, the views on the other side of the trail make up for it: Expect a surprisingly diverse environment of swamps, active cattle farms, and citrus groves. Spanish moss hangs from the trees, and dragonflies and butterflies flit as you work your

The covered bridge located near the southern terminus of the Fort Fraser Trail

Location
Polk

Endpoints
FL 540/Winter Lake Road and US 98 (Lakeland) to FL 60 and US 98 (Bartow)

Mileage
7.75

Type
Rail-Trail

Roughness Index
1

Surface
Asphalt

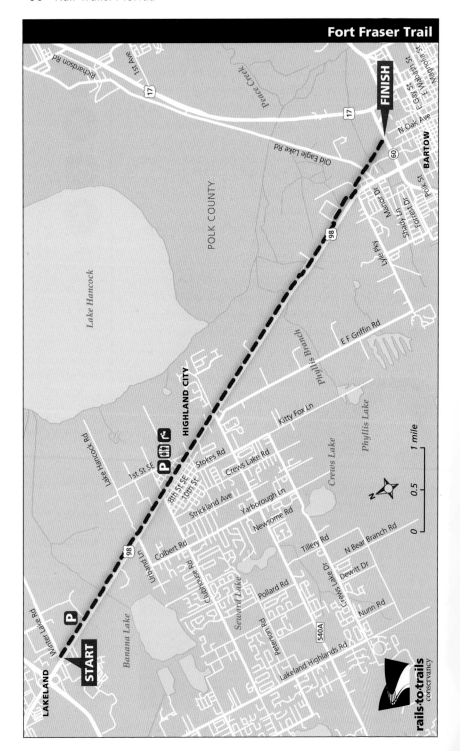

way down the trail. Famous quotes stationed on the overhead electric utility poles (and later in the ground after the wires cross the highway) may inspire you on your journey, while mile markings on the pavement help you keep track of your progress. Interpretive signs with information on the robust history of the area also make regular appearances along the way. One such sign marks the approximate location of the trail's namesake: a short-lived fort built in 1837 during the Second Seminole War. Notably, future president Zachary Taylor served as commander of the fort during this time.

In Highland City, located just north of the former fort's location, the main trailhead offers drinking fountains, restrooms, parking (both car and bike), and picnic tables. Shelters with benches line the trail throughout its route, but this is your only opportunity to fill up your water bottle along the way. South of the trailhead, the route continues as before, although a small forest and covered bridge near the trail's southern terminus at US 98 in Bartow provide both shade and visual interest. A series of big-box stores along US 98 offers an opportunity to grab a bite to eat or shop before gearing up for your return trip back up the trail.

CONTACT: friendsoftheparks.net

DIRECTIONS

To reach parking near the trail's northern endpoint from I-4, take Exit 27 for FL 570 toward Lakeland/Winter Haven (toll road). Head 9.5 miles east on FL 570, and take Exit 10 for US 98 toward Lakeland/Bartow (toll road). Turn right (south) onto US 98/Bartow Road, and continue 0.8 mile. Turn left onto Autumnwood Grove Blvd. (Polk State College entrance). Follow signs for the Polk State College trailhead, located behind the sheriff's office.

To reach the Highland City trailhead from Exit 10 off FL 570, continue south on US 98 2.5 miles to Highland City. Turn left onto Clubhouse Road, and then in 0.2 mile turn right onto Third St. S.E. In 0.1 mile turn right onto Central Ave.; the trailhead and parking are immediately ahead. (Signs for the Highland City trailhead are visible beginning at Third St. S.E.)

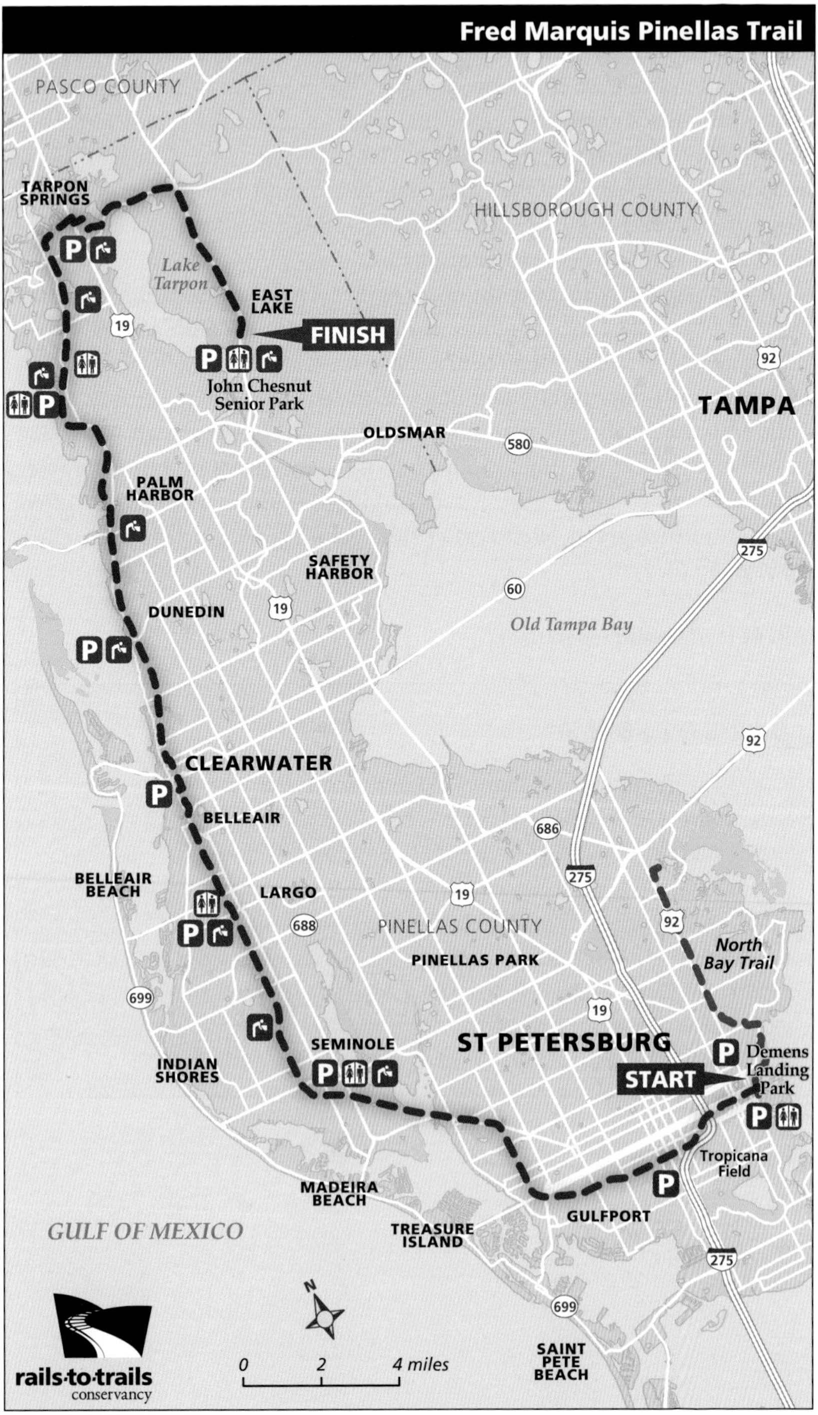

Fred Marquis Pinellas Trail

PASCO COUNTY

HILLSBOROUGH COUNTY

TARPON
SPRINGS

Lake
Tarpon

EAST
LAKE

FINISH

John Chesnut
Senior Park

OLDSMAR

TAMPA

PALM
HARBOR

SAFETY
HARBOR

DUNEDIN

Old Tampa Bay

CLEARWATER

BELLEAIR

BELLEAIR
BEACH

LARGO

PINELLAS COUNTY

PINELLAS PARK

North
Bay Trail

SEMINOLE

ST PETERSBURG

START

Demens
Landing
Park

INDIAN
SHORES

Tropicana
Field

MADEIRA
BEACH

TREASURE
ISLAND

GULFPORT

GULF OF MEXICO

rails·to·trails
conservancy

0   2   4 miles

N

SAINT
PETE
BEACH

One of Florida's most popular urban pathways, the Fred Marquis Pinellas Trail stretches north from St. Petersburg to East Lake, connecting several county parks, coastal areas, and communities. Its multiple access points, mile markers, and parking areas make the trail—and the communities it connects—popular destinations among cyclists.

The trail begins in downtown St. Petersburg at a connection with the busy North Bay Trail on the city's Tampa Bay waterfront. From this point, the unsigned trail travels west as a two-way protected bike lane and sidewalk for 1 mile. Shops, restaurants, and unique landmarks, including the home of the Tampa Bay Rowdies professional soccer team and the Florida Holocaust Museum, are within easy reach from this section of the trail. At Tropicana Field, home to the Tampa Bay Rays,

The popular Pinellas Trail is an urban pathway connecting multiple parks, coastal areas, and communities.

Location
Pinellas

Endpoints
North Bay Trail/Demens Landing Park at First Ave. S.E. and Bayshore Drive S.E. (St. Petersburg) to John Chesnut Sr. Park on E. Lake Road near Sandy Point Road (East Lake)

Mileage
44.3

Type
Rail-Trail

Roughness Index
1

Surface
Asphalt

the shared off-road trail begins. Continuing west, you'll find active industrial businesses and the restored Historic Seaboard Train Station at 22nd Street, which serves as studio space for clay artists.

Near 34th Street (US 19), the trail serves Gibbs High School; note that the pathway can become crowded just before and after school hours. A trail bridge crosses the highway here. The next 15 miles contain dozens of such bridges with sweeping views of the urban landscape, the most scenic of which is the 0.25-mile Cross Bayou Bridge spanning Boca Ciega Bay.

Continue north through Largo, Clearwater, and Dunedin. In downtown Clearwater, the trail transitions to wide sidewalks and a two-way protected bike lane. Use caution here, as the trail crosses roads with heavy traffic.

Farther north, Dunedin offers a particularly pleasant scene, with shops, restaurants, public restrooms, and parking. The Gulf of Mexico is just two blocks away and worth the brief detour for lovely coastal scenery. After passing through the quiet community of Palm Harbor, you'll enter Tarpon Springs's quaint business district, where the trail runs down the middle of Safford Avenue, still separated from car traffic. Past downtown, a newer trail extension turns south on the east side of US 19 and works its way through neighborhoods to Keystone Road. At the end of the route, the trail parallels Keystone Road and East Lake Road, wrapping around the edge of Lake Tarpon. Although the lake is never within sight, small ponds and swamps offer limited aquatic views.

The difficult navigation through shopping centers and neighborhood roads and driveways over the last 5 miles is worth it, as the trail ends at beautiful John Chesnut Sr. Park. The 255-acre county park features a dog park, softball field, playgrounds, and hiking trails, in addition to ample parking, restrooms, and drinking fountains. Continue on foot to view Lake Tarpon, as well as the vast array of wildlife that calls the park home, including hawks, turtles, and alligators.

CONTACT: pinellascounty.org/trailgd

DIRECTIONS

To reach the southern trailhead at Demens Landing Park in St. Petersburg from I-275, take Exit 22 for I-175 E. toward Tropicana Field. Continue on I-175 E. 0.9 mile, and then merge onto Fifth Ave. S./Dali Blvd. In 0.3 mile turn left onto First St. S.E., and go 0.3 mile. Turn right onto First Ave. S. E., directly into the parking lot and trailhead.

To reach the trailhead at John Chesnut Sr. Park from St. Petersburg, take I-275 N. to Exit 30 (FL 686 W./Roosevelt Blvd.), and follow signs for 118th Ave. N. Take the exit ramp and 118th Ave. N. 2.6 miles to 49th St. N., and turn right. In 1.9 miles continue straight on County Road 611, and go another 12.8 miles. Turn left into John Chesnut Sr. Park just after the bridge over Brooker Creek. To reach the trailhead at John Chesnut Sr. Park from I-75, take Exit 275 for FL 56. Head west on FL 56, and go 1.3 miles. Continue on FL 54 W. 14 miles, and turn left onto Trinity Blvd. After 5.5 miles, turn left onto E. Lake Road N., and continue 5.5 miles. Turn right into the park; the trailhead is immediately to your right. For parking, continue along the access road, and turn right. Look for the parking lot on your right.

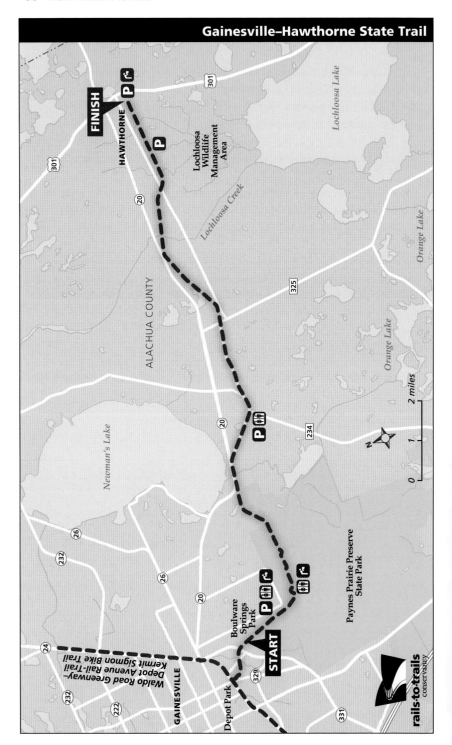

Gainesville–Hawthorne State Trail

This rail-trail runs from the bustling university town of Gainesville to sleepy Hawthorne, through some of Florida's finest terrain. While the trail is a bit hillier than the other rail-trails in the state, it is still quite flat along most of its route. Its 16.5-mile length makes it perfect for a day trip, and the state preserve through which it runs—Paynes Prairie, one of Florida's most treasured natural areas—provides ample opportunities for wildlife spotting, plant identification, and photography. Be sure to take time to walk around the preserve and read about the flora and fauna that call this region home.

Arguably one of the trail's best features is its abundance of amenities; regular trailheads and benches dot the route. The path is paved for its entire length, although you may encounter a horse and rider on the adjacent grassy path; side trails for equestrians snake off from the trail in

Interpretive signs dot the route of the Gainesville-Hawthorne State Trail along Paynes Prairie Preserve State Park.

Location
Alachua

Endpoints
S.E. Depot Ave. and S. Main St. (Gainesville) to S.E. 218 Terrace near S.E. 71st Ave. (Hawthorne)

Mileage
16.5

Type
Rail-Trail

Roughness Index
1

Surface
Asphalt

many directions. A trailhead is under construction at Depot Park in Gainesville; however, the trail is currently accessible at its western end from Boulware Springs Park. Heading south, you'll reach the Paynes Prairie Overlook and, after 2 miles, Paynes Prairie Preserve State Park. After heavy rain flooded the Paynes Prairie Basin in the early 1870s, it boasted a thriving lake with routine steamboat activity until 1891, when a sinkhole drained the basin, leaving behind a mixed landscape of prairie, marsh, and open water.

Several trailside overlooks offer views of the prairie, home to bison, wild horses, and alligators. Park regulations ban visitors from feeding the alligators, and dogs are not permitted, even if leashed (rangers strictly enforce these rules). A half mile into the park, a side trip on the La Chua Trail leads to another viewing area (bicycles are not permitted on this unpaved spur). The gentle, rolling terrain of Paynes Prairie yields to flat trail as riders approach Hawthorne. The trees create a tunnellike canopy over the trail, and the pathway stretches out in straight segments that create vanishing points toward the end of the corridor.

Flanking the easternmost portion of the trail (from just east of Rochelle to Hawthorne) on its south side is the 11,000-acre Lochloosa Wildlife Management Area—part of the Great Florida Birding Trail—home to turkeys, quails, sandhill cranes, and numerous other migratory birds. At its westernmost point, the trail connects with the Waldo Road Greenway–Depot Avenue Rail-Trail–Kermit Sigmon Bike Trail (see page 161).

CONTACT: floridastateparks.org/trail/Gainesville-Hawthorne

DIRECTIONS

To reach the trailhead at Boulware Springs from I-75, take Exit 382 for FL 121 toward FL 331/Gainesville/Williston. Head east on FL 121 N./S.W. Williston Road (signs for Gainesville). In 4.5 miles, turn right onto S.E. Fourth St., which turns slightly left and becomes S.E. 21st Ave. In 0.6 mile turn right onto S.E. 15th St. After 0.6 mile, turn right into Boulware Springs Nature Park.

To reach the trailhead in Hawthorne from I-75, take Exit 382 for FL 121 toward FL 331/Gainesville/Williston. Head east on FL 121 N./S.W. Williston Road (signs for Gainesville). In 4.9 miles, turn right onto S.E. 11th Ave. In 0.3 mile turn left onto S.E. 15th St. In 0.2 mile turn right onto S.E. Eighth Ave., and drive 0.7 mile. Turn right onto FL 20 E./S.E. Hawthorne Road, and drive 13.4 miles. Turn right onto S.E. 215th Terrace and then left onto 65th Ave. in quick succession. Turn right onto 218th St. Drive 0.4 mile, and turn left onto S.E. 71st Ave. Turn right at the first cross street, which dead-ends into the trailhead parking lot.

General James A. Van Fleet Trail runs a straight 29-mile course through some of Florida's most scenic rural landscape. If you are looking to immerse yourself in wetlands and wildlife, the Van Fleet Trail will not disappoint; at least one-third of the trail runs through Central Florida's Green Swamp, a 322,690-acre wetland.

Horseback riding is welcome on the trail; however, the trail operators ask that horses keep to the 5-foot mowed shoulder along each side of the trail and that proof of negative Coggins is available.

The trail stretches from Polk City to the town of Mabel on FL 50. The Polk City trailhead has ample parking, picnic and restroom facilities, and an expansive field of clipped green grass perfect for a game of pickup soccer.

The General James A. Van Fleet State Trail is one of Florida's most rural paved rail-trails.

Location
Lake, Polk, Sumter

Endpoints
Berkley Road and Commonwealth Ave. (Polk City) to County Road 772 and S.E. 121st Ave. (Mabel)

Mileage
29

Type
Rail-Trail

Roughness Index
1

Surface
Asphalt

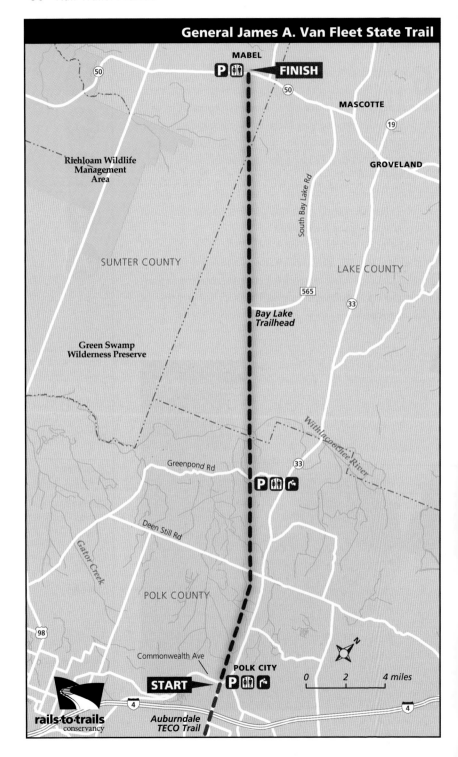

General James A. Van Fleet State Trail

MABEL

P 🚻   ◀ **FINISH**

50

50

MASCOTTE

19

Richloam Wildlife
Management
Area

GROVELAND

South Bay Lake Rd

SUMTER COUNTY

LAKE COUNTY

565

33

*Bay Lake
Trailhead*

**Green Swamp
Wilderness Preserve**

Withlacoochee River

Greenpond Rd

33

P 🚻 🚲

Deen Still Rd

Gator Creek

POLK COUNTY

98

Commonwealth Ave

POLK CITY

P 🚻 🚲

START ◀

0   2   4 miles

rails-to-trails
conservancy

*Auburndale
TECO Trail*

The rail-trail's flat and arrow-straight route, with one slight curve around mile marker 5, has made it a favorite among time-trial bicyclists. But because of its isolated and rural setting, you are unlikely to encounter many trail users besides the occasional speedster.

As you approach the Green Pond Road trailhead around mile marker 10, you enter the Green Swamp, one of Florida's protected wetland and wildlife areas. On the right day, you may encounter feral pigs, armadillos, buzzards, and possibly an alligator or two soaking up the warmth of the trail's asphalt surface.

Bay Lake trailhead signals the end of the protected wildlife reserve, although the last 10 miles of your journey toward the Mabel trailhead, and the trail's end, are equally scenic. While it may be tempting to race back to Polk City, savoring your return trip along this beautiful, serene trail is rewarding too.

CONTACT: **floridagreenwaysandtrails.com**

DIRECTIONS

To Polk City trailhead: from I-4, take Exit 44 for FL 559 toward Polk City/Auburndale (0.3 mile), and head north on FL 559 N. Continue 0.6 mile, and turn left to stay on FL 559 N. After 1.8 miles, turn left onto Commonwealth Ave. N./FL 33. In 0.2 mile turn right onto Berkley Road. Almost immediately, before the road curves south, you will see the trailhead and parking area in a small park just north of Berkley Road. Although there is an information kiosk and a playground, there are no amenities such as restrooms and drinking water at the northern end. (Parking is available for people with disabilities.)

To Green Pond Road trailhead: From I-4, take Exit 58 toward Poinciana/Kissimmee. Head west on ChampionsGate Blvd., and go 0.9 mile. Turn right onto Loughman Road/Ronald Reagan Pkwy./Deen Still Road, and go 12.6 miles. Turn right onto FL 33, and go 4.8 miles. Turn left onto Green Pond Road, and go 2 miles to the trailhead, on your right.

To Mabel trailhead: Take I-75 to Exit 301 for US 98/FL 50. Head east on US 98/FL 50, and go 19 miles. Turn right onto S.E. 121st Ave. to reach the trailhead parking.

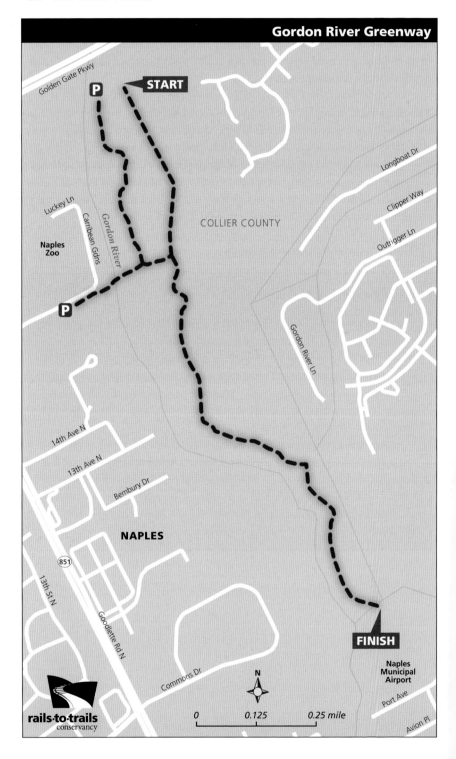

Gordon River Greenway offers an easy and convenient taste of the Florida wild through a 126-acre natural area in the heart of Naples. The 12-foot-wide pavement is ultra smooth and winds through a mixture of palm trees, pine flatwoods, and scrubland. The trail is interspersed with elevated boardwalk sections over wetlands, where you can watch for birds, tortoises, and other wildlife. Bump-outs on bridge crossings over the Gordon River provide spots to fish or simply enjoy the views.

The trail is lush, green, and well maintained, with frequent covered benches to stop and take in the sights. Open daily until 10 p.m., the trail is also well lit and provides a safe atmosphere for nighttime excursions. Several access points with parking, bike racks, restrooms, and drinking fountains make the trail manageable for trail users of most

The boardwalk-like Gordon River Greenway winds through the wetlands of Naples.

Location
Collier

Endpoints
Golden Gate Pkwy., 0.5 mile west of Goodlette-Frank Road, to Naples Municipal Airport near Port Ave. and North Road (Naples)

Mileage
1.7

Type
Greenway/Non-Rail-Trail

Roughness Index
1

Surface
Asphalt, Boardwalk

ages and abilities. Situated nearby, the Naples Zoo and a canoe and kayak launch offer additional opportunities for outdoor recreation.

The first phase of the trail opened in 2014. When complete, the pathway will continue farther south to Central Avenue in Old Naples. Future plans call for extending the trail north to Freedom Park (just past Golden Gate Parkway) and southeast to a developing trail that will loop around Naples Municipal Airport.

CONTACT: **gordonrivergreenway.org**

DIRECTIONS

To reach the northern trailhead, take I-75 to Exit 105 for County Road 886/Golden Gate Pkwy. Head west on CR 886/Golden Gate Pkwy., and go 3 miles to the entrance to Gordon River Greenway Park on your left (the south side of the roadway).

Historic Jungle Trail winds nearly 8 miles through the hammock and mangrove habitats of Florida's barrier islands north of Vero Beach. The trail—really a road—was built in the 1920s to support the citrus industry and is on the National Register of Historic Places. The trail accommodates vehicle traffic but is used primarily by cyclists, walkers, and joggers. The route is sandy (some places can get soft or are prone to flooding), but a majority of the surface is hard packed and easygoing for wide-tire bicycles.

Begin on the northern end in Vero Beach at the Pelican Island National Wildlife Refuge—the nation's first—which was established in 1903 by Teddy Roosevelt. Parking is available along the trail to your left, just off FL A1A. You'll find restrooms and drinking fountains here, as well as access to a 2.5-mile walking path that circles a nearby peninsula (to your right) on the Indian River.

The Historic Jungle Trail winds through hammock and mangrove habitats in Florida's barrier islands.

Location
Indian River

Endpoints
FL A1A near Seaview Blvd. (Vero Beach) to FL A1A at Old Winter Beach Road (Indian River Shores)

Mileage
7.8

Type
Greenway/Non-Rail-Trail

Roughness Index
2

Surface
Sand

Historic Jungle Trail

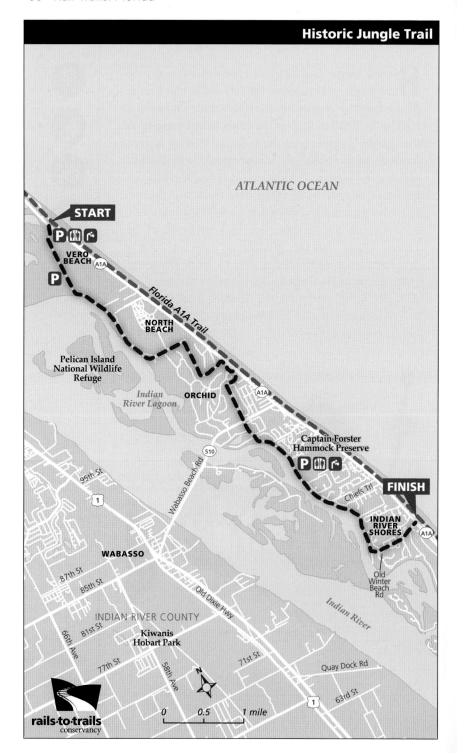

ATLANTIC OCEAN

START

VERO BEACH   A1A

Florida A1A Trail

NORTH BEACH

Pelican Island National Wildlife Refuge

Indian River Lagoon

ORCHID   A1A

Captain Forster Hammock Preserve

510

Wabasso Beach Rd

95th St

1

Chiefs Trl

FINISH

INDIAN RIVER SHORES   A1A

WABASSO

87th St
85th St
81st St
66th Ave
77th St
58th Ave

Old Dixie Hwy

INDIAN RIVER COUNTY

Kiwanis Hobart Park

71st St

Old Winter Beach Rd

Indian River

Quay Dock Rd

1   63rd St

N

0   0.5   1 mile

rails·to·trails
conservancy

Head south about 0.5 mile in an open savanna of palm, sea grape, and other coastal wetland species, and you'll reach a turnoff (left) to another parking area and access to the Centennial Trail (walking only, wheelchair accessible, bike racks available). The part-paved, part-boardwalk trail leads to a hiking spur, as well as a lookout to the original Pelican Island (the refuge has expanded greatly since 1903).

Continuing on the Historic Jungle Trail, you'll travel a stretch of the Indian River Lagoon with access points for kayaking, canoeing, and fishing (check local regulations), and wind through the region's hammock habitat. After leaving the refuge, you'll begin to spy gated golf course communities. This stretch is more shaded; however, note that the surface may be covered in debris left by local vegetation-trimming crews.

When you reach the crossing for Orchid Island Drive, proceed with caution; the vegetation can block your view. A short distance later, you'll reach another crossing at FL 510/Wabasso Beach Road. Use caution when crossing here as well, as there are no pedestrian signals.

The next section along the Indian River is much less shady; you'll see mangroves along the shore to the west and backyards of upscale homes to the east. You may also see a manatee or two in the river as well as large blue land crabs scurrying into their burrows. At Captain Forster Hammock Preserve, take a side trip through the 110-acre area, which offers nature trails, parking, bike racks, restrooms, and drinking fountains.

Near its southern terminus, the trail turns into the paved Old Winter Beach Road for about 0.5 mile and terminates at FL A1A. As an alternative to heading back north on the Historic Jungle Trail, you can pick up a side path to your left, the Route A1A Trail, which extends north 6 miles to the wildlife refuge.

CONTACT: ircgov.com

DIRECTIONS

To reach the Vero Beach access point and parking from I-95, take Exit 156 for County Road 512 toward Sebastian/Fellsmere. Head east on Fellsmere Road (signs for Sebastian), and drive 1.9 miles. Continue on Sebastian Blvd. 0.6 mile. Turn right onto 90th Ave. After 1.2 miles, continue on 85th St. another 4.7 miles. Continue on FL 510 E. 2.6 miles. Turn left (north) onto FL A1A and drive 3.8 miles; you will see a sign on the right indicating Pelican Island Wildlife Refuge. Turn left onto the road marked Historic Jungle Trail, and turn left into the parking lot.

To reach the southern terminus, take the directions above until you come to the intersection of FL 510 and FL A1A, and turn right onto FL A1A. Head south 2.4 miles to Old Winter Beach Road, and turn right. Drive a short distance to the bend in the road. The trail starts on the right when the road becomes gravel/sand. There is no public parking available at the southern terminus.

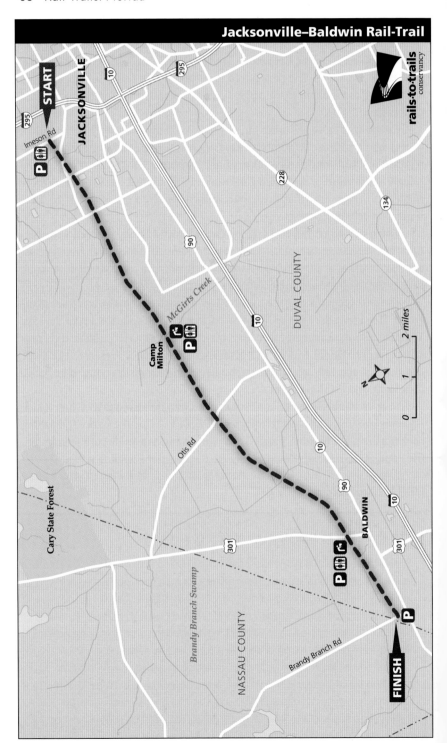

Located west of Jacksonville's downtown core, the Jacksonville-Baldwin Rail-Trail provides 14.5 miles of multiuse pathway with a variety of landscapes, including wetlands, forests, and cornfields. The route, built on a former CSX right-of-way, crosses the McGirts and Brandy Branch Creeks as it extends west to the small town of Baldwin. Plans are in the works to connect the trail to neighboring recreational and ecological corridors.

The trail contains some low-traffic crossings, a well-maintained surface, and plenty of shade, making for a low-stress user experience. Amenities dot the route, including benches, restrooms, and picnic tables.

Less than 6 miles from the Imeson Road trailhead is the Camp Milton Historic Preserve (1225 Halesma Road), a key Florida Civil War site accessible from the trail by a rail-trail connector spur. The preserve contains several

Scenic landscapes and a well-maintained pathway make for a pleasant, low-stress user experience on the Jacksonville-Baldwin Rail-Trail.

Location
Duval

Endpoints
Imeson Road near Tia Road (Jacksonville) to Brandy Branch Road/ County Road 121 near Carter St. (Baldwin)

Mileage
14.5

Type
Rail-Trail

Roughness Index
1

Surface
Asphalt

interpretive trails, Civil War relics, boardwalks, a restored farmhouse from 1889, and "The American Forest," consisting of trees created from specimens found at Civil War sites. Signs describing these features, as well as Florida Civil War history, can be found throughout the preserve. You'll also find bathrooms, water fountains, and parking.

Lucky visitors may spot wildlife such as turkeys, alligators, rabbits, gophers, tortoises, and coral snakes. Beware of the latter—a venomous species with wide black and red bands broken by narrow yellow rings. Birding is especially good at Camp Milton; be on the lookout for eastern bluebirds, eastern meadowlarks, palm warblers, loggerhead shrikes, bald eagles, American kestrels, and sharp-shinned hawks.

The Baldwin Station visitor center, located 12.5 miles from the Imeson Road trailhead, is a pleasant place to take a break, use a restroom, and get water. A skate park is also nearby. Trail users will find plenty of restaurants, convenience stores, and gas stations near the trail's eastern endpoint in Jacksonville, as well as at its terminus in Baldwin.

CONTACT: tinyurl.com/jacksonvillebaldwinrt

DIRECTIONS

To reach the Imeson Road trailhead (1800 Imeson Road) from I-295, take Exit 22 for Commonwealth Ave., and continue northwest on Commonwealth Ave. 1.1 miles. Turn right onto Imeson Road. Turn left into the parking lot; the trailhead will be to your right.

To reach the Baldwin trailhead from I-10, take Exit 343 toward Baldwin, and head north on US 301. Follow US 301 1.1 miles, and turn left onto US 90/W. Beaver St. After 1.5 miles, turn right onto Brandy Branch Road. Turn right into the trailhead parking lot.

You'll find John Yarbrough Linear Park Trail to be an unexpected surprise in Fort Myers. Although bound by busy streets in all directions, the corridor itself is green and serene. The paved trail rolls alongside Ten Mile Canal for 6 miles and crosses over it on a few pedestrian bridges where you can stop and take in the views. Look for egrets, herons, and other birds wading through the lush vegetation, and eagles in the tall treetops. You might even get lucky and spot an alligator.

The canal was built in the 1920s to control flooding in the southern part of the city, and when the trail's first section opened in 2005, it was named Ten Mile Linear Park after the waterway. Later, it was renamed to honor a longtime director of Lee County Parks and Recreation, which owns and operates the trail. Portions of the trail can

The John Yarbrough Linear Park Trail, paralleling the lush Ten Mile Canal, offers a natural oasis in Fort Myers.

Location
Lee

Endpoints
Six Mile Cypress Pkwy. near Independence Circle to Colonial Blvd., 0.25 mile west of Southland Court (Fort Myers)

Mileage
6

Type
Rail-with-Trail

Roughness Index
1

Surface
Concrete

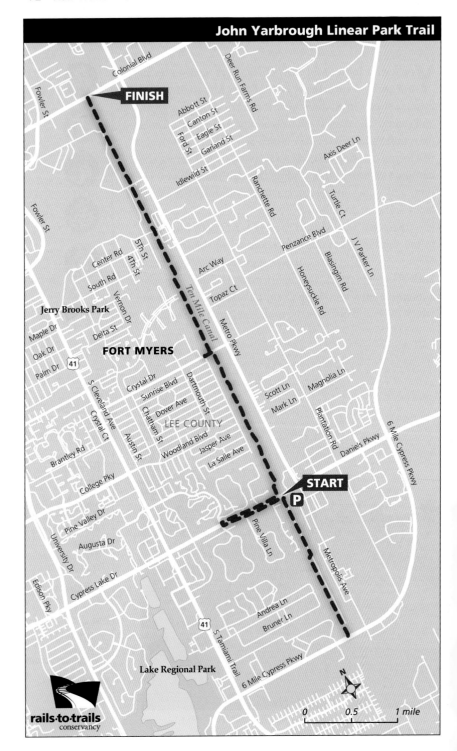

John Yarbrough Linear Park Trail

FINISH

START

P

Fowler St
Colonial Blvd
Deer Run Farms Rd
Abbott St
Carlton St
Eagle St
Ford St
Garland St
Axis Deer Ln
Idlewild St
Ranchette Rd
Turtle Ct
Fowler St
Penzance Blvd
J V Parker Ln
5th St
4th St
Center Rd
South Rd
Arc Way
Blasingim Rd
Honeysuckle Rd
Vernon Dr
Topaz Ct
Ten Mile Canal
Jerry Brooks Park
Maple Dr
Delta St
Metro Pkwy
Oak Dr
41
Palm Dr
FORT MYERS
Crystal Dr
Sunrise Blvd
Dartmouth St
Scott Ln
Magnolia Ln
S Cleveland Ave
Chatham St
Dover Ave
Mark Ln
Crystal Ct
Austin St
Woodland Blvd
Jasper Ave
LEE COUNTY
Plantation Rd
Daniels Pkwy
6 Mile Cypress Pkwy
Brantley Rd
La Salle Ave
College Pky
Pine Valley Dr
Pine Villa Ln
Metropolis Ave
University Dr
Augusta Dr
Edison Pky
Cypress Lake Dr
Andrea Ln
Bruner Ln
41
S Tamiami Trail
Lake Regional Park
6 Mile Cypress Pkwy

N

rails·to·trails
conservancy

0   0.5   1 mile

be found along both banks of the canal, and those on the west side are built on the former Seaboard Air Line Railroad.

You'll find dedicated trail parking only on the southern end of the trail on the south side of Daniels Parkway, so begin there and follow the path north. At multiple points along the trail, you'll encounter covered picnic tables that provide shelter from the hot sun or cool rain, both of which are likely on any given day in Florida.

The northern end of the trail opens up, and over a median of brush, you'll be able to see the train cars of the Seminole Gulf Railway, which the trail parallels. In addition to serving freight, the rail line also hosts murder mystery dinner trains several nights a week. The trail ends at Colonial Boulevard, and just on the other side of the roadway is Colonial Station (a departure point for trains). If you need refreshment at the end of your journey, a few chain restaurants are accessible via the narrow, paved pathways heading both east and west along the boulevard.

CONTACT: tinyurl.com/johnyar

DIRECTIONS

To reach the parking lot at the trail's midpoint, take I-75 to Exit 131 for Cape Coral and Daniels Pkwy. Head west on Daniels Pkwy., and go 3.6 miles. Look for the small trail parking lot on the south side of Daniels Pkwy. just before the railroad crossing. (You'll know you're getting close when you see the canal on your right with a small pedestrian bridge over it.)

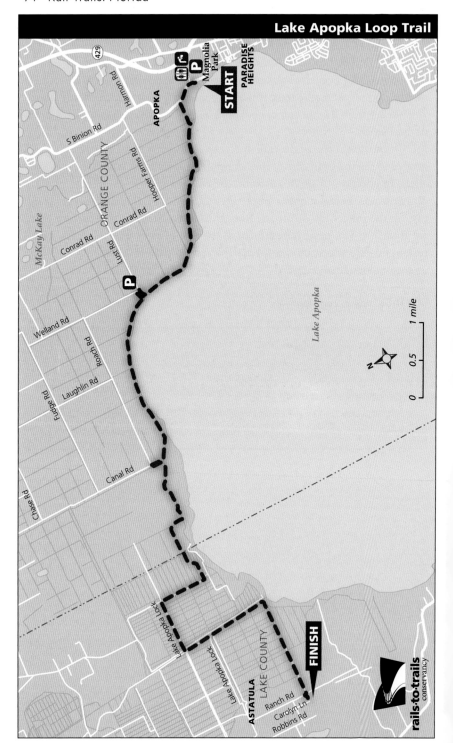

This trail follows the edge of Lake Apopka, giving trail users an opportunity to see the vast array of wildlife Florida has to offer. Be sure to bring your binoculars; the total number of bird species observed on the north shore of the lake is 348, which is among the highest count in the state for a local area. The trail's rough path (a mountain or hybrid bike is recommended) encourages you to slow down and get in touch with nature. The first thing you'll notice after leaving the Magnolia Park trailhead on the eastern side of the lake is a small sign warning you to look out for alligators. After 4 miles, you'll come to a historic

The Lake Apopka region is known for having one of the highest counts of bird species in Florida.

Location
Lake, Orange

Endpoints
Magnolia Park on Binion Road, 0.25 mile north of Sheaf Road (Apopka), to Clay Island trailhead on Carolyn Lane, 0.2 mile south of Peebles Drive (Astatula)

Mileage
14.6

Type
Greenway/Non-Rail-Trail

Roughness Index
3

Surface
Asphalt, Crushed Stone

pump house with a picnic area, restrooms, and an overlook of the lake; occasionally, you can see great blue herons and glossy ibis fishing here.

If you enter the trail from the Clay Island trailhead on the western side of the lake, you'll come to an observation tower that provides excellent views of the lake and wildlife below. Continuing along the trail, you'll see canals that were created in 1987 to help clean the lake and act as a passageway for life below the surface.

Whichever direction you choose, this wildlife-filled trail offers great sights and plenty of opportunities to take photographs. After exploring the Lake Apopka Loop Trail, check out the nearby 22-mile West Orange Trail, east of the Magnolia Park trailhead.

CONTACT: orangecountyparks.net

DIRECTIONS

To access the Magnolia Park trailhead from I-4, take Exit 90 or 90B for FL 414/Maitland Blvd. Follow signs for FL 414 W./Lake Destiny Drive N. Merge onto FL 414 W./Maitland Blvd., and continue 9.3 miles on FL 414 W. (toll road). Take Exit 4B to merge onto FL 429 S. toward Tampa (toll road), and go 1.8 miles. Exit toward County Road 437A/Ocoee Apopka Road, and turn right onto CR 437/S. Binion Road. After 0.6 mile, turn left into the trailhead.

To access the Clay Island trailhead from I-4, take Exit 90 or 90B for FL 414/Maitland Blvd. Follow signs for FL 414 W./Lake Destiny Drive N. Merge onto FL 414 W./Maitland Blvd., and continue 13.6 miles on FL 414 W. (toll road). Take the Orange Blossom Trail exit. Turn left, and in 0.3 mile turn right onto US 441 N./W. Orange Blossom Trail. Go 3.6 miles, and turn left onto W. Jones Ave., which turns into Duda Road. In 3.7 miles turn left onto CR 448A, and in 0.5 mile turn right onto CR 48. After 3.2 miles, turn left onto Ranch Road; drive 1 mile, and then turn left to stay on Ranch Road 0.2 mile. Turn right onto Robbins Road. After 1.2 miles, turn left onto Peebles Drive and then right onto Carolyn Lane. The trailhead will be directly in front of you. There is no formal designated parking area here.

Lake Okeechobee Scenic Trail (also known as LOST) is a 110-mile trail circumnavigating the seventh-largest freshwater lake in the United States. LOST's location on top of the levee offers expansive views and opportunities to spot birds, including egrets, herons, osprey, and many southerly migrating species in the winter.

Lake Okeechobee is renowned for its bass fishing and is a major destination for boating, featuring spectacular sunsets. Alligators and manatees can be spotted in the water; you may also spot an alligator that found its way onto the shore, so be cautious. The trail passes near several small agricultural communities based primarily on cattle ranching and sugarcane production.

Originally built by the U.S. Army Corps of Engineers along the top of flood-control levees, many sections of the trail have been paved. A challenge to experiencing the trail is that many sections have been subject to long closures

Venture through LOST for some expansive views of Lake Okeechobee.

Location
Glades, Hendry, Martin, Okeechobee, Palm Beach

Endpoints
US 98, FL 78, and US 27 circling Lake Okeechobee (South Bay to Okeechobee and Port Mayaca to Lakeport)

Mileage
110

Type
Rail-Trail

Roughness Index
1–2

Surface
Asphalt, Gravel

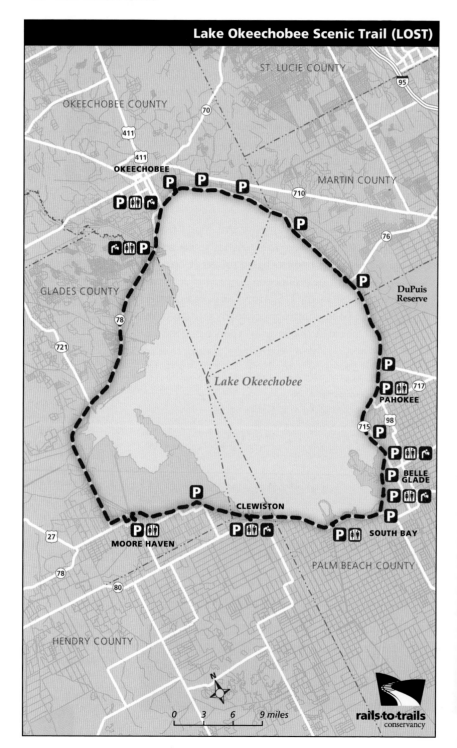

for maintenance of the levee's culverts, mainly on the southern half of the levee shoreline. As of the publication of this guidebook, approximately half of the trail is closed to recreation and is not expected to reopen until 2019. Despite the closures, there are long sections of open, separated trails around the northern half of the lake. Before embarking on a trip along the LOST, it is highly recommended to check current trail conditions and closures by calling the U.S. Army Corps of Engineers' office.

There are numerous campgrounds around the lake. For motels and dining, Okeechobee, on the north side of the lake, offers the most opportunities. There are also options on the south side of the lake, particularly in Moore Haven, Clewiston, and Belle Glade. The small but notable Clewiston Museum is a worthwhile detour for its exhibits of the area's natural and cultural history, including fossils of a mastodon and a saber-toothed tiger.

CONTACT: 1.usa.gov/1udYpIV; U.S. Army Corps of Engineers: **863-983-8101**

DIRECTIONS

To access the eastern trailhead at Port Mayaca from I-95, take Exit 101 for FL 76 toward Stuart/Indiantown. Head southwest on FL 76/S.W. Kanner Hwy., and go 25.3 miles (the road will curve left when you reach the water, and then curve inland). Make a sharp left onto US 98 N., and drive 1.1 miles. Pass a bridge and turn left. Turn right toward the small trailhead parking lot.

To access the northern trailhead in Okeechobee from I-95, take Exit 129 for FL 70/Okeechobee Road. Head west on FL 70, and go 32 miles. Turn left onto US 441 N./US 98 N. Go 3.1 miles, and turn right onto FL 78. Immediately turn left up a sloped road where a brown sign indicates the way to LOST; the trail is at the top.

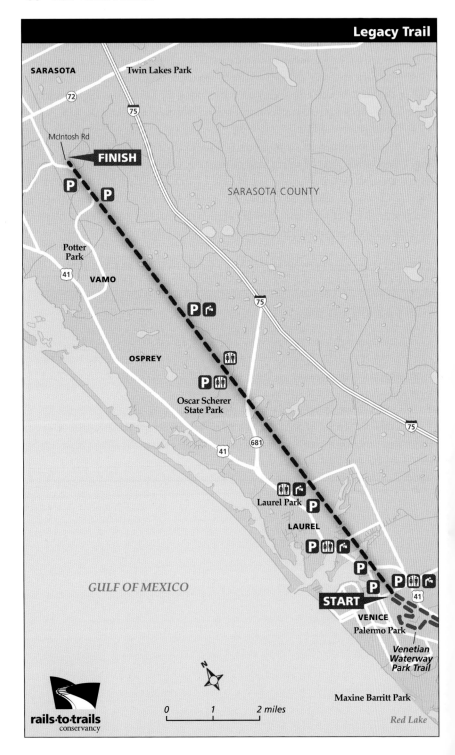

Legacy Trail

Legacy Trail has a splendid opening: the Historic Venice Train Depot, a pale sunset-orange structure that fits into the beachy pastel palette for which Florida is known. Situated adjacent to a waterway dotted with palm trees, the Mediterranean Revival–style building dates to 1927 and was once considered the finest station on the line. Open year-round on Saturdays during select hours, the inside contains displays about the Seaboard Air Line Railroad, on which the rail-trail was built. Ringling Bros. and Barnum & Bailey Circus used the tracks to reach its winter headquarters in Venice from 1960 to 1992; next to the depot stands a bronze statue of circus star Gunther Gebel-Williams, who is heralded as "The Greatest Wild Animal Trainer of All Time."

The smooth, paved trail unfurls north from the depot and is an easy ride for bicyclists: It is level and straight

The Historic Venice Train Depot offers a beautiful start to the Legacy Trail.

Location
Sarasota

Endpoints
Historic Venice Train Depot at E. Venice Ave. and N. Seaboard Ave. (Venice) to McIntosh Road near Prosperity Circle (Sarasota)

Mileage
10.7

Type
Rail-Trail

Roughness Index
1

Surface
Asphalt

for just over 10 miles to the outskirts of Sarasota, with only a few well-marked street crossings on low-volume roads. The only steep spot comes at the US 41 pedestrian overpass; you'll want to shift gears for an easier ride here. Several other smaller bridge crossings over waterways offer picturesque views. Much of the trail is exposed, but shaded benches with drinking fountains appear nearly every mile, making the experience comfortable. Multiple trailheads with free parking also make the route customizable, with easy opportunities for getting on and off the trail.

At the midway point, the trail traverses sprawling Oscar Scherer State Park, which offers ample opportunities for outdoor recreation, including camping, hiking, canoeing, and kayaking along South Creek, as well as fishing and swimming in Lake Osprey.

As in much of the state, nature is close at hand along the trail; you're likely to see many types of birds, lizards, snakes, tortoises, and rabbits. Watch for the many interpretive signs to identify and learn more about the regional flora and fauna, as well as the area's history.

Should you have extra time and energy, explore the 8.6-mile Venetian Waterway Park Trail, which heads south from the Historic Venice Train Depot to Caspersen Beach (known for the prehistoric shark teeth that wash up on shore) and continues back up the other side of the Gulf Intracoastal Waterway.

CONTACT: scgov.net/parks/pages/legacytrail.aspx

DIRECTIONS

The Historic Venice Train Depot (303 E. Venice Ave.) at the southern terminus of the trail offers parking, restrooms, and drinking water. Take I-75 to Exit 195 toward Venice/Laurel. Head east on Laurel Road, and go 2.8 miles. Turn left onto US 41/Tamiami Trail, and go 3.3 miles. Turn right onto E. Venice Ave. Keep right, and in 0.2 mile just before you reach the Gulf Intracoastal Waterway, turn right into the depot parking lot. The depot also serves as a stop for the Sarasota County Area Transit bus system.

Six other trailheads, offering additional parking and amenities, are available as you head north on the trail.

Lehigh Greenway Rail Trail, which runs alongside the Lehigh Canal, offers a scenic journey on a former rail spur of the Lehigh Portland Cement Company.

The post–World War II construction boom prompted the Pennsylvania-headquartered Lehigh Cement Company to expand its operations, and a cement plant was opened in Flagler County, Florida. The eastern end of the trail is located on the switchyard for the former cement plant, from which rail cars traveled west to link up with the Florida East Coast Railway in Bunnell.

A good place to begin your journey is at the eastern terminus of the trail, located at the southeast corner of the Graham Swamp Conservation Area on Colbert Lane, just north of Harbor View Drive. A long, wooden bridge at the start of the trail cuts through the preserve, which features hiking paths and a 7-mile mountain biking trail.

A pleasant 6.6-mile journey awaits cyclists on the Lehigh Greenway Rail Trail.

Location
Flagler

Endpoints
Graham Swamp Conservation Area at Colbert Lane and Harbert View Drive (Palm Coast) to Royal Palms Pkwy. and US 1 (Bunnell)

Mileage
6.6

Type
Rail-Trail

Roughness Index
1

Surface
Asphalt

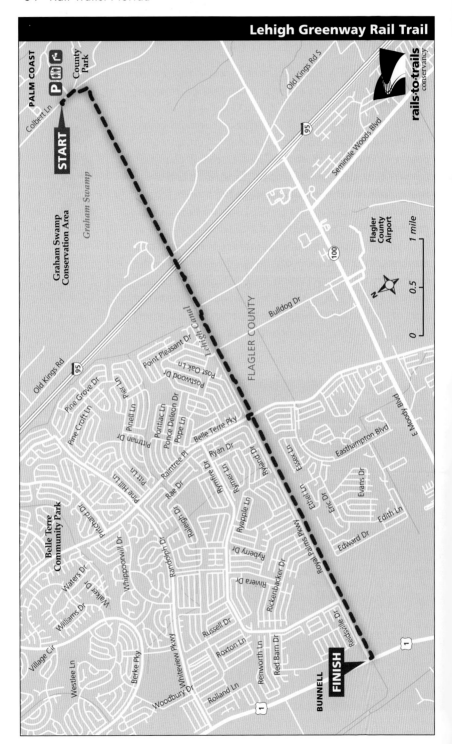

Lehigh Greenway Rail Trail

The trail skirts along its edge for the first 2 miles, providing scenic views of a Florida swamp forest, after which you'll cross three intersections in quick succession. This section of trail offers clearer views of the canal, Spanish moss–filled trees, and native fauna, such as egrets hunting for lunch.

Bicycle maintenance stations are available along the trail at two access points from Royal Palms Parkway. The trail ends at the intersection of Royal Palms Parkway and US 1.

CONTACT: flaglercounty.org/facilities.aspx

DIRECTIONS

To reach the Colbert Lane trailhead from I-95, take Exit 284 for FL 100 E./E. Moody Blvd. (signs for Flagler Beach). Head east on FL 100/E. Moody Blvd. 1.9 miles, and turn left onto Colbert Lane. After 1.8 miles, the trailhead will be on your left, just past Harbor View Drive.

In addition to the Colbert Lane trailhead, there are three access points from the sidewalk of Royal Palms Pkwy. and one access point from Old King Road, which intersects the trail. The western trailhead is located at the corner of Royal Palms Pkwy. and US 1. (No parking is available at this endpoint.)

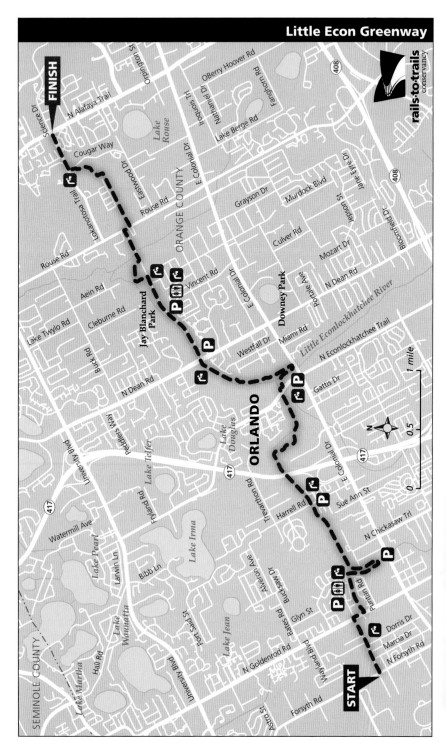

This popular trail, which hosts as many as 50,000 people per month, has a variety of amenities, making it a great family and group destination. You can enjoy canoeing or kayaking along the canal or play a game of soccer, tennis, or basketball. The waterside shelters provide a place to relax and watch osprey and red-shouldered hawks glide over the water.

Starting at the trail's western end at North Forsyth Road, the atmosphere is suburban, but you are quickly transported to a more rural setting when you reach the Little Econlockhatchee (Econ) River, which provides excellent opportunities for fishing and bird-watching via several small bridges. The long, sweeping turns and open space encourage you to stop and admire Florida's beautiful landscape.

Toward the middle of the route, close to East Colonial Drive (to your right), the trail travels over a short wooden bridge and cuts left down and toward the water, where you can see alligators and iguanas.

The open space along the Little Econ Greenway offers many opportunities to admire the beautiful Florida landscape.

Location
Orange

Endpoints
N. Forsyth Road near Partridge Lane to N. Alafaya Trail and Science Drive (Orlando)

Mileage
8

Type
Greenway/Non-Rail-Trail

Roughness Index
1

Surface
Asphalt

Continuing east, you'll pass a track and field belonging to Union Park Middle School, which also maintains a butterfly garden. Then you'll reach Jay Blanchard Park at North Dean Road. The park is a hot spot for recreational activity, with tennis and basketball courts, large sports fields, a playground, picnic benches, and lots of trees for shade. A YMCA, located near the park entrance, operates a pool for members.

As you near the eastern terminus, the trail takes on a suburban feel similar to its western end. On the right, you'll pass University High School, where you might catch a baseball game from the outfield. The trail ends across the street from a Walgreens.

After exploring the Little Econ Greenway, check out the nearby 6.5-mile Cady Way Trail and 22.8-mile Cross Seminole Trail, west and north of North Forsyth Road, respectively. The Little Econ Greenway will eventually connect the Cady Way Trail to the University of Central Florida. Future phases of the Little Econ Greenway will also link to the Cross Seminole Trail, creating a loop of active-transportation and recreational opportunities.

CONTACT: orangecountyparks.net

DIRECTIONS

Note: There are no parking lots or street parking at the trail endpoints.

To access the western endpoint on N. Forsyth Road from I-4 E., take Exit 83A for FL 50. Merge onto N. Garland Ave., and in 0.2 mile turn right onto Colonial Drive/FL 50. In 5.7 miles turn right onto N. Forsyth Road. The trailhead is 0.6 mile north, at Partridge Lane. From I-4 W., take Exit 84 and turn left onto Colonial Drive/FL 50. Follow the rest of the directions above.

The closest parking lot for the western endpoint is located at the end of Lady Frances Way at Arcadia Acres Park Soccer Field. To reach this access point from I-4, head east on Colonial Drive, and go 6.2 miles. Turn left onto FL 551/Goldenrod Road, and drive 0.5 mile. Turn right onto Liverpool Blvd., and after 0.3 mile, turn right onto Merlin St. and then left onto Lady Frances Way. Look for the parking lot straight ahead and trail access on the right.

To access the eastern endpoint from I-4, take Exit 82A for FL 408. Head east on FL 408 (toll road), and go 10.5 miles as the road turns into Challenger Pkwy. Turn right onto N. Alafaya Trail/FL 434. The trail endpoint will be 0.7 mile ahead on the left at the corner of N. Alafaya Trail and Lokanotosa Trail.

The closest parking lot for the eastern endpoint is in Jay Blanchard Park. To reach the park from I-4, take Exit 82A for FL 408. Head east on FL 408 (toll road), and continue 9 miles. Take Exit 19 for Dean Road. Turn left onto N. Dean Road (partial toll road), and turn right onto Jay Blanchard Trail after 2.2 miles. Turn left into the parking lot at Jay Blanchard Park.

One of Florida's oldest rail-trails, the 9.4-mile M-Path Trail is located underneath Miami-Dade Transit's MetroRail, making it a rail-with-trail. Together with the passenger rail service, the trail greatly enhances the reach of the transit service to nearby neighborhoods, business centers, hospitals, and other points of interest in the community. MetroRail allows bicycles to be brought aboard trains for no additional charge, and stations along the trail are located at Brickell, Vizcaya, Coconut Grove, Douglas Road, University, South Miami, and Dadeland (two stops). The trail route can be confusing to follow because it passes through some of the southern MetroRail stations; remember that the trail follows underneath the raised rail platform to stay on course.

The M-Path parallels US 1 (South Dixie Highway) for almost the entire length of the trail, crossing 28 roadways and running through some of the most urbanized space in

The 9.4-mile M-Path Trail is located underneath Miami-Dade Transit's MetroRail, making it a rail-with-trail.

Location
Miami-Dade

Endpoints
S.W. First Ave. and the Miami River to Dadeland Mall at US 1 and S.W. 88th St. (Miami)

Mileage
9.4

Type
Rail-with-Trail

Roughness Index
1

Surface
Asphalt, Concrete

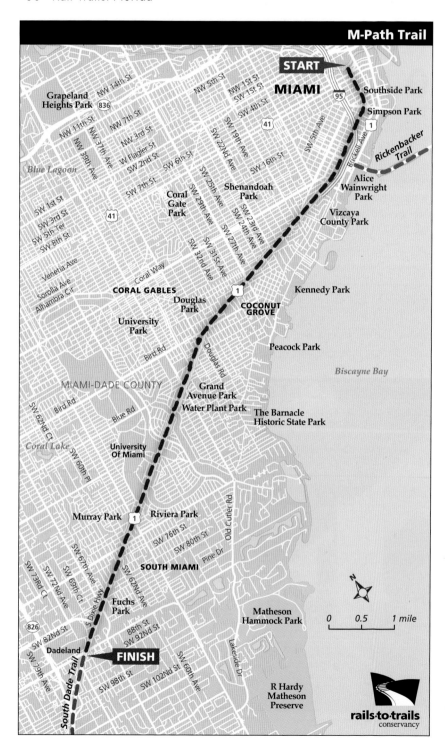

M-Path Trail

START

MIAMI

Southside Park

Simpson Park

Rickenbacker Trail

Alice Wainwright Park

Vizcaya County Park

Grapeland Heights Park

Blue Lagoon

Coral Gate Park

Shenandoah Park

CORAL GABLES

Douglas Park

University Park

Kennedy Park

COCONUT GROVE

Peacock Park

Biscayne Bay

MIAMI-DADE COUNTY

Grand Avenue Park

Water Plant Park

The Barnacle Historic State Park

University Of Miami

Coral Lake

Murray Park

Riviera Park

SOUTH MIAMI

Fuchs Park

Matheson Hammock Park

Dadeland

FINISH

R Hardy Matheson Preserve

South Dade Trail

N

0   0.5   1 mile

rails·to·trails
conservancy

all of Florida. Amenities are located throughout the length of the trail, and you are never far from restaurants and services. One of South Florida's most visited bike shops, Mack Cycles and Fitness—which offers a large fleet of bike rentals—is located just off the trail and to the right on Sunset Drive. Businesses have started to redevelop and offer access from the trail, and this trend is expected to continue.

Miami-Dade County has been focusing resources on making the crossings safer by improving intersections and adding bridges at the busiest road crossings. In areas where there are few intersections, the trail becomes more of a parklike amenity.

Starting from the northern endpoint at the Miami River, you quickly reach a large overpass and a tree canopy. Just before the Vizcaya MetroRail Station, you can cut left onto a short trail bridge to cross over I-95 and exit the trail. If you head right off the trail, you can turn left onto Southwest 32nd Road and head about two blocks to South Miami Avenue. If you turn right here, you'll come to the Vizcaya Museum and Gardens. Toward the southern end of the trail is the University of Miami and South Miami Hospital, after which the trail terminates at Dadeland Mall.

The M-Path is a designated part of the East Coast Greenway alignment and is becoming an important backbone in the region's trail network. Together with the South Dade Trail, it forms a 31-mile system based on the old Flagler Railroad line that once carried passengers all the way down the Florida Keys to Key West. Via a short and newly improved bike lane, individuals can also connect to the Rickenbacker Trail (see page 120), which extends from Alice Wainwright Park (just off where US 1 and South Miami Avenue meet) to Key Biscayne.

CONTACT: friendsofmpath.org

DIRECTIONS

The trail can be accessed at all MetroRail stations and numerous roadway intersections along the route. Metered parking and restrooms for fare-ticket holders are available at all MetroRail stations.

To access the northern endpoint at the Miami River, take I-95 to Exit 1B toward US 41/S.W. Eighth St./Brickell Ave. Merge onto S.W. Third Ave. (if heading northbound on I-95) or S.W. Fourth Ave. (if heading southbound on I-95). Head east on US 41, and continue 0.2 mile. Turn left onto S.W. First Ave., where you will find a small amount of street parking, though the endpoint is actually on US 41.

To access the southern endpoint from I-95 heading south in Miami, continue 7.5 miles on US 1. Make a slight right onto S.W. 88th St. The trail endpoint is to your right, where S.W. 88th St. and Pinecrest Pkwy. meet. There is no formal trail parking at this trailhead.

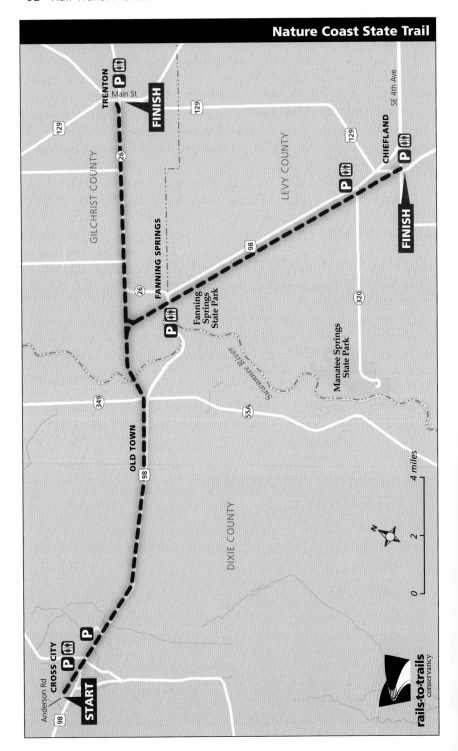

One of the Sunshine State's best-kept trail secrets, the Nature Coast State Trail connects five small rural towns—Cross City, Old Town, Fanning Springs, Trenton, and Chiefland—along a T-shaped, 32-mile corridor. The Atlantic Coast Railroad once traversed this pathway carrying timber, crops, and passengers throughout the Suwannee River Valley.

Today, visitors can connect to its railroad history by exploring three historic depots and an old railroad trestle. The well-maintained, flat trail (open daily, 8 a.m.–sunset) boasts a diversity of agricultural scenery and wildlife, as well as views of the Suwannee River, historical landmarks, parks, springs, and trailside amenities. Equestrians can access the trail at either the Old Town or Fanning Springs trailheads, where trailer parking is provided.

Starting at the farthest northwest leg of the trail from Cross City to Old Town, take note of the historic white Cross City railroad depot (adjacent to the trail), which

Equestrians can access the Nature Coast State Trail in Old Town and Fanning Springs.

Location
Dixie, Gilchrist, Levy

Endpoints
Anderson Road and Continental Road (Cross City) to N. Main St./US 129 and N.W. Fourth Ave. (Trenton) or S.E. Fourth Ave./ FL 345 and S.E. Second St. (Chiefland)

Mileage
32

Type
Rail-Trail

Roughness Index
1

Surface
Asphalt

dates back to the early 1900s. Traveling east past Old Town, pause at viewing areas along the old railroad trestle spanning the Suwanee River. You can spot manatees in the river below during the cooler months.

The less traveled section east from Old Town leads to the quaint town of Trenton, which has a trailhead, restrooms, antiques shops, restaurants, and a colorful railroad mural. Don't miss the Old Trenton Train Depot, a historic downtown landmark.

Visitors to the base of the T-shaped trail from Fanning Springs to Chiefland are afforded an amazing trailside diversion to Fanning Springs State Park, located at the Fanning Springs trailhead. Its clear-water springs, where you can swim or snorkel, have attracted visitors for thousands of years. Birding opportunities abound, with red-shouldered hawks, woodpeckers, and barred owls frequenting the park.

At the trailhead in Chiefland, you will discover another historic train depot and a farmers market (open every second and fourth Saturday except in July and August, when it's closed). Not to miss is nearby Manatee Springs State Park (west of Chiefland), which features a first-magnitude spring boasting an average of 100 million gallons of clear, cool water daily. In the winter, West Indian manatees swim upriver to the warmer waters of the springs, which are also popular for snorkeling, scuba diving, canoeing, and kayaking. The state has acquired a 9-mile corridor that will extend the Nature Coast State Trail from the Trenton depot trailhead east toward Newberry.

CONTACT: floridastateparks.org/trail/nature-coast

DIRECTIONS

To reach the Cross City trailhead from I-75, take Exit 387 toward Newberry. Head west on FL 26 W./W. Newberry Road, and drive 32.3 miles. Take a slight right onto US 19 N./US 98 N. After 13.6 miles, turn right (north) onto S.E. 259 St. The parking lot is immediately to your left. The trail extends northwest another mile to the trailhead. (There is no parking available at the western terminus.)

To reach the Trenton trailhead from I-75, take Exit 387 toward Newberry. Head west on FL 26/W. Newberry Road, and drive 24.9 miles. Turn right (north) onto N.W. First St., and in 0.1 mile turn left at the old train depot into a small parking lot.

To reach the Chiefland trailhead from I-75, take Exit 384 for FL 24 toward Gainesville/ Archer, and head southwest on FL 24/S.W. Archer Road. Follow FL 24 W. 17.7 miles, and turn right onto N.E. 90th St./Ishie Ave. After 2.5 miles, turn right onto Alternate US 27 N., and continue 11.3 miles. Turn left onto FL 345 S./S.E. Fourth Ave.; after 0.9 mile, turn right onto S. Main St. In 0.2 mile turn right onto S.E. Second Ave.; the trailhead and parking are immediately to your right at the old train depot (Chiefland Chamber of Commerce).

Markham Park near FL 84 and Weston Road (Sunrise) to S. University Drive/FL 817 and FL 84 (Plantation): 7.5 miles

The New River Greenway offers a straight route along the North New River Canal, which runs between the greenway and I-595. Despite its location in a densely developed area near an interstate, the trail provides a pleasant respite from traffic, offering a valuable connection between neighborhoods and surprising opportunities for up-close wildlife viewing. Egrets and herons are common here, as are iguanas, which often dart across the trail. Be sure to note the trail signs, which advise users to be mindful of alligators and snakes.

The New River Greenway provides valuable connections among local neighborhoods and a pleasant respite from traffic for walkers and bikers.

Location
Broward

Endpoints
Markham Park near FL 84 and Weston Road (Sunrise) to S. University Drive/FL 817 and FL 84 (Plantation); Sewell Lock at FL 84 and Davie Road (Davie) to S.W. 22nd Terrace and FL 84 (Fort Lauderdale)

Mileage
11.5

Type
Greenway

Roughness Index
1

Surface
Asphalt

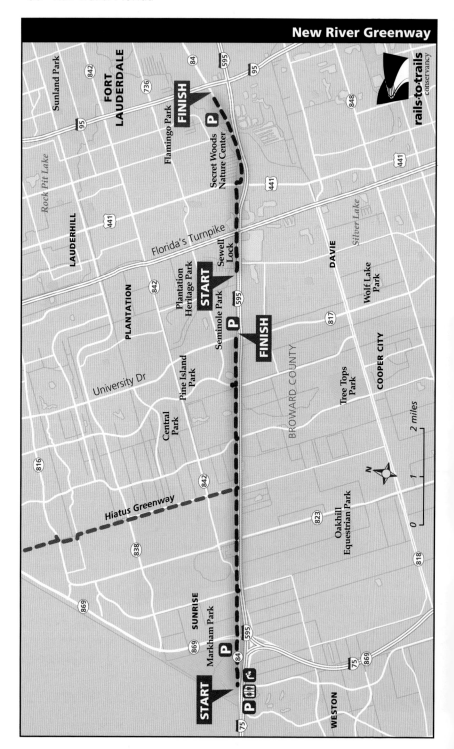

Markham Park, located at the west end of the western trail segment, is a prime local recreation destination. Encompassing nearly 700 acres, the park features an impressive range of facilities, including a disc golf course, an archery range, an observatory, and a model-airplane field. The park also includes a network of mountain bike trails, including some designed for adaptive riders. Mountain bikers also have the option of continuing along the trail beyond Markham Park to the Conservation Levee Greenway, an unpaved doubletrack trail extending 24 miles. Currently, users have to go out and back; ultimately, it will become part of a 32-mile regional greenway system that will extend deep into the Everglades Wildlife Management Area.

There are several places near the trail to stop for food and beverages (including a shopping center just west of University Drive, accessible via Southwest 78th Avenue; note the bike rack). However, the corridor is mostly residential. Be prepared for a number of inconvenient intersection crossings, several of which span major streets. Signs direct users off the trail to cross the canal at traffic signals and then direct users back onto the trail.

The recently completed Hiatus Greenway offers a pleasant detour and an option for a long trip on the trail, extending another 5 miles to the north along the west side of the C-42 Canal. You can access the Hiatus Greenway just west of where the New River Greenway crosses South Hiatus Road.

Sewell Lock at FL 84 and Davie Road (Davie) to S.W. 22nd Terrace and FL 84 (Fort Lauderdale): 4 miles

The eastern segment of the New River Greenway begins at Sewell Lock in Davie and extends east along the canal to Southwest 22nd Terrace in Fort Lauderdale, a distance of about 4 miles. At 6–8 feet in width, this section of the trail is considerably narrower than its western counterpart. To reach this segment, cross to the eastern side of University Drive and turn right (you'll pass under I-595). Turn left onto the sidewalk along FL 84. Follow the sidewalk 1.5 miles to Davie Road and turn left (you'll cross back under I-595). There is an access point to the Greenway directly ahead.

Near the eastern endpoint is the Secret Woods Nature Center, a 57-acre urban wilderness area. Highlights include a butterfly garden and two nature trails that meander through marshes with native Florida vegetation and abundant wildlife. Parking is also available here for trail users.

CONTACT: broward.org/greenways

Markham Park, located at the west end of the western trail segment, is a prime local recreation destination. Encompassing nearly 700 acres, the park features an impressive range of facilities, including a disc golf course, an archery range, an observatory, and a model-airplane field. The park also includes a network of mountain bike trails, including some designed for adaptive riders. Mountain bikers also have the option of continuing along the trail beyond Markham Park to the Conservation Levee Greenway, an unpaved doubletrack trail extending 24 miles. Currently, users have to go out and back; ultimately, it will become part of a 32-mile regional greenway system that will extend deep into the Everglades Wildlife Management Area.

There are several places near the trail to stop for food and beverages (including a shopping center just west of University Drive, accessible via Southwest 78th Avenue; note the bike rack). However, the corridor is mostly residential. Be prepared for a number of inconvenient intersection crossings, several of which span major streets. Signs direct users off the trail to cross the canal at traffic signals and then direct users back onto the trail.

The recently completed Hiatus Greenway offers a pleasant detour and an option for a long trip on the trail, extending another 5 miles to the north along the west side of the C-42 Canal. You can access the Hiatus Greenway just west of where the New River Greenway crosses South Hiatus Road.

Sewell Lock at FL 84 and Davie Road (Davie) to S.W. 22nd Terrace and FL 84 (Fort Lauderdale): 4 miles

The eastern segment of the New River Greenway begins at Sewell Lock in Davie and extends east along the canal to Southwest 22nd Terrace in Fort Lauderdale, a distance of about 4 miles. At 6–8 feet in width, this section of the trail is considerably narrower than its western counterpart. To reach this segment, cross to the eastern side of University Drive and turn right (you'll pass under I-595). Turn left onto the sidewalk along FL 84. Follow the sidewalk 1.5 miles to Davie Road and turn left (you'll cross back under I-595). There is an access point to the Greenway directly ahead.

Near the eastern endpoint is the Secret Woods Nature Center, a 57-acre urban wilderness area. Highlights include a butterfly garden and two nature trails that meander through marshes with native Florida vegetation and abundant wildlife. Parking is also available here for trail users.

CONTACT: broward.org/greenways

DIRECTIONS

To western segment: To access the Markham Park endpoint from I-595, exit toward FL 869/ Sawgrass Expy., and then follow signs to exit at FL 84/Weston Road. Head west on FL 84. After 0.4 mile, turn right onto Markham Park Road. The endpoint is immediately to your right, after the canal. To reach parking, take the first right onto Markham Park Road, and loop right and then left. When you reach a four-way intersection, turn right (this is the access road for the park). Look for a parking lot on your right.

To access the Plantation trailhead from I-95, take Exit 26 for FL 736/Davie Blvd. Head west on FL 736 W./Davie Blvd. 5.1 miles (the road becomes S.W. 12th St./Peters Road). Find the trailhead by turning left onto FL 817/S. University Drive and continuing 0.4 mile to where the road meets the canal. No parking is available here. To find parking from FL 817, pass S. University Drive, and in another 0.1 mile turn left onto S.W. 78th Ave. After 0.4 mile, you'll see an access point to the trail. On-street parking spaces are in the area.

To eastern segment: To access parking at the eastern end of the trail at Secret Woods Nature Center from I-95, take Exit 25 for FL 84/Marina Mile Road. Head west on FL 84/Marine Mile Road, and drive 0.5 mile. Turn right (north) into the park entrance.

North Bay Trail provides a beautiful journey around the edge of Tampa Bay in St. Petersburg, with abundant views of the crystal-clear water and access to neighborhoods, shops, and parks throughout. At the trail's southern end, a seamless connection to the Pinellas Trail offers further opportunities to explore St. Petersburg and Pinellas County. From its beginning in the north at Riviera Bay Park, the trail heads south over a small waterway to First Street. The next several miles parallel the suburban roadway, with thousands of homes, apartments, stores, and schools within easy reach; be mindful of the dozens of unsignaled street and driveway crossings at this point in the journey.

The experience improves significantly at Coffee Pot Park, a neighborhood facility situated at the top of Coffee Pot Bayou. The trail is wedged between brick-surfaced Coffee Pot Boulevard and the water south of the park, with

A beautiful journey around the edge of Tampa Bay awaits on the North Bay Trail.

Location
Pinellas

Endpoints
Riviera Bay Park at 81st Ave. N.E. and Macoma Drive N.E. to Fred Marquis Pinellas Trail in Demens Landing Park at First Ave. S.E. and Bayshore Drive N.E. (St. Petersburg)

Mileage
6.3

Type
Greenway/Non-Rail-Trail

Roughness Index
1

Surface
Concrete

the Old Northeast neighborhood's beautiful waterfront homes in a mix of architectural styles on one side and their accompanying boat docks on the other. Be sure to take some time to look into the bayou; its shallow waters are a popular manatee feeding ground.

Soon the trail enters the sprawling open space of a series of waterfront parks, including Flora Wylie Park, Gizella Kopsick Palm Arboretum, North Shore Park, and Vinoy Park. All offer stunning views of Tampa Bay, with colorful birds and palm trees common along the route. Bicyclists should be prepared to yield to the many pedestrians on the trail who can be found gazing off into the bay or simply taking in the fresh air.

The trail continues to hug the shoreline as it heads south, although a sharp turn at the historic (and bright pink) Vinoy Park Hotel should be taken with caution. As you proceed to the trail's southern endpoint, consider stopping at the city's Museum of Fine Arts or Museum of History—both trailside—or watching the boats come and go from the St. Petersburg Marina. At Demens Landing Park, the trail ends, but a seamless connection to the Pinellas Trail on First Avenue enables much more travel throughout the city and beyond.

CONTACT: stpete.org/parks_and_recreation/city_trails

DIRECTIONS

To reach the southern trailhead at Demens Landing Park in St. Petersburg from I-275, take Exit 22 for I-175 E. toward Tropicana Field. Continue on I-175 E. 0.9 mile, and then merge onto Fifth Ave. S./Dali Blvd. In 0.3 mile turn left onto First St. S.E., and go 0.3 mile. Turn right onto First Ave. S.E., directly into the parking lot and trailhead.

To reach the trail's northern endpoint at Riviera Bay Park from I-275, take Exit 30 for FL 686/Roosevelt Blvd. Head southeast on FL 686/Roosevelt Blvd., and drive 1.3 miles. Turn left onto Gandy Blvd., and immediately turn right onto US 92/Fourth St. In 1.1 miles turn left onto 83rd Ave. After 0.5 mile, turn right onto Macoma Drive. Parking for the park and trail is on the left.

Ocean Boulevard Path

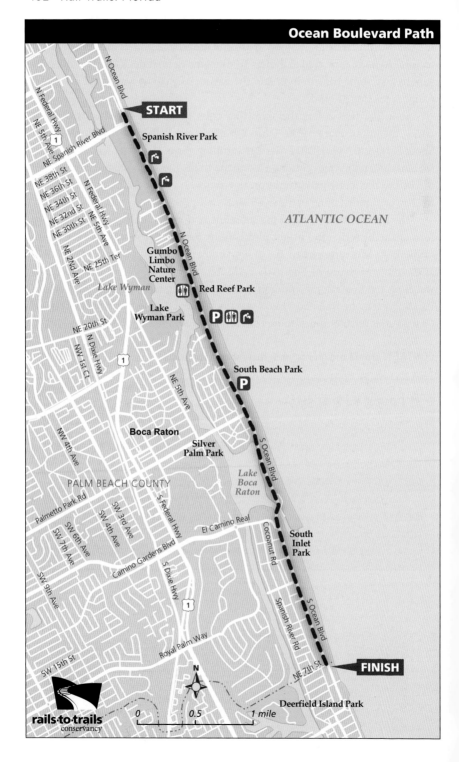

Ocean Boulevard Path runs adjacent to Ocean Boulevard, extending from Northeast Spanish River Boulevard to Northeast Seventh Street in Boca Raton. The path is notable for its four parks: Spanish River Park, Red Reef Park (which, despite its name, no longer has a reef), South Beach Park, and South Inlet Park. All four parks have beach access, and Spanish River and Red Reef Parks also offer picnic areas on the west side of Ocean Boulevard. Accessing the beaches via the trail can save you quite a bit on parking fees, which tend to be high in this area.

The trail offers partial ocean views at several locations and meanders into the trees at Spanish River Park. While development along this section of Ocean Boulevard is almost entirely residential, there are commercial areas with eateries a short distance away from the south end of

The Ocean Boulevard Path is notable for its local parks.

Location
Palm Beach

Endpoints
N.E. Spanish River Blvd. and FL A1A/Ocean Blvd. to N.E. Seventh St. and FL A1A/Ocean Blvd. (Boca Raton)

Mileage
4.7

Type
Greenway/Non-Rail-Trail

Roughness Index
1

Surface
Asphalt

the trail on Palmetto Park Road. Otherwise, you can bring your own food and take advantage of one of the many picnic areas available in the parks.

Other than the beaches, a real highlight of the trail is the Gumbo Limbo Nature Center, located about a third of the way down the trail. Gumbo Limbo is a unique facility for learning about the region's natural environment—particularly its marine life—and features educational exhibits, an outdoor aquarium, and a sea turtle rehabilitation facility. Gumbo Limbo also has a short nature trail and butterfly garden and offers a range of programming for children.

It is important to point out that there is a notable gap in the trail. Three miles south of the trail's starting point at Spanish River Boulevard, the trail narrows to a sidewalk as it approaches and crosses the bridge over the Boca Raton Inlet. On the south side of the bridge, there is only a southbound bike lane (and no sidewalk) for about 500 feet until the trail resumes south of East Camino Real, continuing another mile until Northeast Seventh Street.

CONTACT: myboca.us/pages/traffic/bicyclespedestrians-maps

DIRECTIONS

Parking is generally expensive at the public beaches in the area; however, there is metered parking at Red Reef Park on the west side of Ocean Blvd. Free parking is available at Gumbo Limbo for nature center visitors only. The trail is located approximately 1 mile east of US 1 and can most easily be reached by one of the main roads that cross the intracoastal waterway: E. Hillsboro Blvd., E. Palmetto Park Road, or N.E. Spanish River Blvd.

To reach the northern endpoint from I-95, take Exit 48A or 48, and head east on FL 794/ Yamato Road. In 1.2 miles turn right onto US 1, and go 0.6 mile. Turn left onto N.E. Spanish River Blvd., and in 0.6 mile turn left onto N. Ocean Blvd. Go 0.3 mile, and make a U-turn (destination will be on the right).

To reach the southern endpoint from I-95, take Exit 42A or 42, and head east on FL 810/ Hillsboro Blvd. In 2.5 miles turn left onto N.E. 20th Ave./N. Ocean Drive. The road immediately turns right and becomes N.E. Second St. Make a slight left onto N.E. 21st Ave. Continue 0.3 mile. Turn left onto N.E. Seventh St. The endpoint is immediately to your right.

Old Cutler Trail runs through some of the most scenic neighborhoods in the greater Miami area. Start your journey at the south end of the trail at the Ronald Reagan Turnpike, just a short water bridge away from the Black Creek Trail to the west. From here, the trail heads northeast along the right side of Old Cutler Road and quickly turns into widened sidewalks with some shopping areas and restaurants. Trail users should proceed with caution through this section, which contains many vehicle crossings.

After a short time on the trail, you'll come to a section framed by beautiful neighborhoods and parks on either side. Note the wondrously large ficus trees with extensive aerial roots that surround the trail; in some instances, the trees create a lumpy trail surface, so stay alert. Due to the trail surface, hybrid or mountain bikes are recommended.

The beauty of the local area is evident along the Old Cutler Trail.

Location
Miami-Dade

Endpoints
Old Cutler Road and
S.W. 224th St. (Cutler
Bay) to Old Cutler Road
and Cocoplum Road
(Coral Gables)

Mileage
11

Type
Greenway/Non-Rail-Trail

Roughness Index
1–2

Surface
Asphalt, Concrete

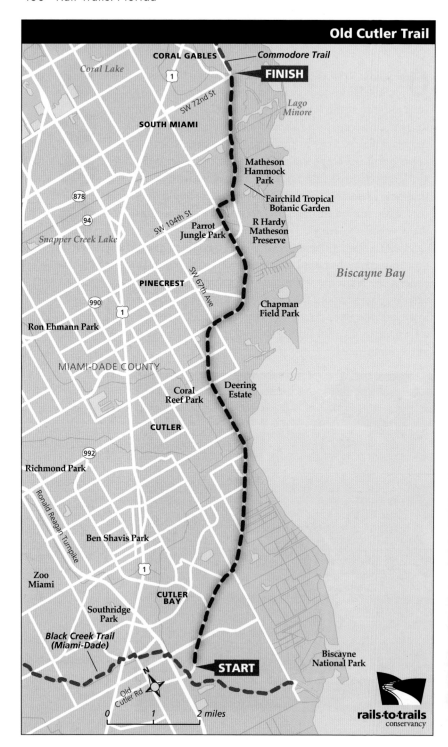

Old Cutler Trail

CORAL GABLES

Coral Lake

Commodore Trail

FINISH

SW 72nd St

Lago Minore

SOUTH MIAMI

Matheson Hammock Park

Fairchild Tropical Botanic Garden

SW 104th St

Parrot Jungle Park

R Hardy Matheson Preserve

Snapper Creek Lake

PINECREST

SW 67th Ave

Biscayne Bay

Ron Ehmann Park

Chapman Field Park

MIAMI-DADE COUNTY

Coral Reef Park

Deering Estate

CUTLER

Richmond Park

Ben Shavis Park

Zoo Miami

CUTLER BAY

Southridge Park

Black Creek Trail (Miami-Dade)

START

Biscayne National Park

Old Cutler Rd

N

0   1   2 miles

rails·to·trails
conservancy

Eventually, the trail curves east, switching to the left side of Old Cutler Road immediately after Southwest 67th Avenue. The trail heads due east 1 mile, then curves left and continues straight along what is known as the Red Road Trail. Before reaching Southwest 104th Street, you'll come to a creek crossing and signs for the Old Cutler Trail to your right; here, the trail drops you onto Snapper Creek Road for a short time until it meets Old Cutler Road again, just after Southwest 53rd Avenue. Cross Old Cutler Road to stay on the trail. You'll pass Fairchild Tropical Botanic Garden on your right, as well as the American Orchid Society, which contains a large collection of flowers to learn about and enjoy, and a large park with picnic tables and a tree canopy filled with many varieties of tillandsia (air plants).

Heading north, more ficus roots grip the walls along the trail, giving the route in this coastal community a unique feel. Other than road crossings and bumpy root patches, the trail is flat and easygoing.

Eventually, the trail ends at a roundabout where Old Cutler Road terminates (just south of Cartagena Park) and the Commodore Trail begins. North of the roundabout, there is a picturesque bridge crossing that connects to Ingraham Terrace Park (and the Commodore Trail), a lush green public space with palm trees, benches, and a circular walkway around a fountain.

CONTACT: www.miamidade.gov/parksmasterplan/library/oct.pdf

DIRECTIONS

To reach the Cutler Bay trailhead from I-95, take I-95 S. to its end, and continue on US 1/S. Dixie Hwy. Go 15.2 miles, and turn left onto Marlin Road. After 1.6 miles (at the T), turn right onto Old Cutler Road. The trail will follow the road; continue 1.2 miles to the trailhead on your left at the intersection of Old Cutler Road and S.W. 224th St. Note that there is no formal trail parking at this endpoint, but limited residential on-street parking is available in the surrounding neighborhoods.

To reach the Coral Gables trailhead from I-95, take I-95 S. to its end, and continue on US 1/S. Dixie Hwy. Go 3.6 miles, and turn left onto S.W. 42nd Ave./Le Jeune Road. In 1.4 miles, pass Ingraham Terrace Park and cross the waterway; look for parking on the traffic circle. The trailhead is at the second exit of the circle at Old Cutler Road.

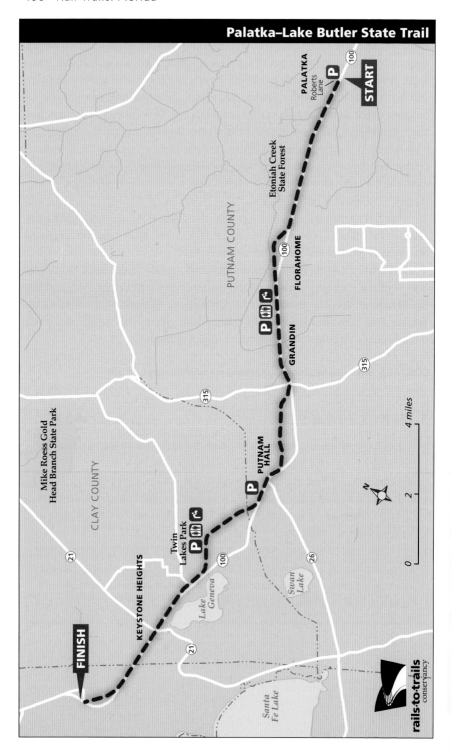

Palatka–Lake Butler State Trail

Opened in 2008, this trail runs through the former Norfolk Southern Railway right-of-way from Palatka to Lake Butler. Currently about 20 miles long, the trail will extend 47 miles when complete. Long-term plans include connecting the trail to a 100-mile trail system that will extend as far as St. Augustine.

A tranquil, shaded ride or walk through nature awaits visitors starting from the Roberts Lane trailhead and moving west. This section runs along Etoniah Creek State Forest for a few miles. Lush greenery, wildflowers, and a few lakes and streams greet travelers along much of the trail. While there is no official parking at the trail's eastern endpoint, there is parking at the Florahome trailhead, where you can enjoy a playground and baseball field and use a self-serve bike repair station. Another pit stop with plentiful parking is at Twin Lakes Park in Keystone Heights,

Tranquility and shade await visitors of the Palatka–Lake Butler State Trail.

Location
Bradford, Clay, Putnam

Endpoints
Roberts Lane and FL 100 (Palatka) to FL 100 near S.E. 66th St. (Keystone Heights)

Mileage
19.7

Type
Rail-Trail

Roughness Index
1

Surface
Asphalt

which boasts picnic tables, soccer fields, tennis courts, and a playground. Each of these locations provides restrooms and water fountains.

The northwestern section of the trail is less scenic, passing through a commercial section of Keystone Heights. Although less aesthetically pleasing, chain stores offer food and supplies.

The completed section of trail is well maintained and paved throughout. Adventurous hikers are permitted to use the yet-to-be-paved sections of trail in the west; however, these areas are not mapped, and many bridges are missing, requiring the use of local roads to avoid these gaps. One planned 4-mile section of trail near Lake Butler is open for use; however, as this guidebook went to press, the segment's surface had not been improved, and it is currently suitable only for hikers and experienced mountain bikers.

CONTACT: floridastateparks.org/trail/palatka-lake-butler

DIRECTIONS

Currently, there is no official parking at either the eastern or western terminus of the trail. For parking on the eastern portion, Florida State Parks recommends the Florahome trailhead. From I-75, take Exit 390 for FL 222 toward Gainesville. Head east on FL 222, and drive 14.1 miles. Continue on FL 26 E 16.9 miles, and turn right onto FL 100 E. Continue 5 miles, and turn left onto Coral Farms Road. Parking is available immediately to your right.

Reach the eastern terminus of the trail by following the directions above to the intersection of FL 26 and FL 100. Turn right onto FL 100 E., and go 11.8 miles. Turn left onto Roberts Lane; the trail is immediately to your left.

Parking is available on the western portion of the trail at the Twin Lakes Park trailhead in Keystone Heights (6065 Twin Lakes Road). To reach the trailhead from I-75, take Exit 390 for FL 222 toward Gainesville. Head east on FL 222, and drive 14.1 miles. Continue on FL 26 E. After 12.1 miles, take a slight left onto County Road 219. Follow it 3.7 miles, and turn left onto FL 100 W. After 1.2 miles, turn right onto S. Twin Lakes Road. In 0.2 mile turn right onto Twin Lakes Road, and go 0.5 mile. Turn right into the entrance for the park. Cross over the trail into the parking lot.

The Palatka–St. Augustine State Trail takes you through serene, easily meandered wooded areas filled with historical and cultural features before passing through a fast-paced area with modern-day amenities as it parallels FL 207, eventually returning to woods for its last couple of miles. Interpretive signage along the trail tells the history of Armstrong and the railroad that once carried fresh produce and other goods to and from St. Augustine more than 130 years ago.

Parking is scarce, so you'll want to begin your journey at an informal parking area located where the trail and FL 207 split, just south of Vermont Heights. You won't want to miss the northern end of the trail, which lies 2 miles north of this starting point. The trail's railroad history is readily apparent as the paved trail ends, abruptly giving way to railroad ties that make for a unique experience.

Serene, wooded areas balance out the more fast-paced segments of the Palatka–St. Augustine State Trail.

Location
St. Johns

Endpoints
1.3 miles north of
FL 207 on Deerpark Blvd.
(Elkton) and FL 207
and County Road 207
(Spuds)

Mileage
8.5

Type
Rail-Trail

Roughness Index
1

Surface
Asphalt

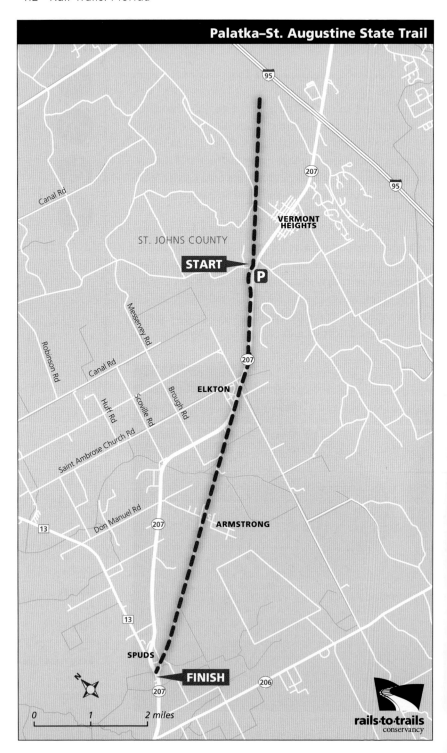

Palatka–St. Augustine State Trail

Doubling back to the informal parking area, the trail parallels FL 207, eventually crossing the highway at a well-marked intersection. You'll pass through a largely wooded section of trail where several nearby streams provide a home for aquatic fauna that you may be able to spot from the trail.

After a few miles, you'll reach Armstrong, a historic African American farming community. Residing here are an estimated 300–400 Gullahs and Geechees—the descendants of West Africans who, from the mid-1700s to the mid-1800s, were enslaved on plantations on barrier islands throughout the southern coastal region and have developed a unique culture and traditions over the past two and a half centuries. Continuing 1 mile, you will reach the southern end of the trail, where it intersects again with FL 207.

Although the trail is only 8.5 miles, additional segments are planned, with a long-term goal of connecting to the Palatka–Lake Butler State Trail for a system encompassing more than 100 miles. The trail will also become part of the 260-mile St. Johns River–to–Sea Loop Trail.

CONTACT: floridastateparks.org/trail/palatka-augustine

DIRECTIONS

There is no vehicle access to the northern terminus and no parking at the southern terminus. An informal parking area is located on a stretch of old highway off FL 207 between the towns of Elkton and Vermont Heights. From I-95, take Exit 311. Head south on FL 207 toward St. Augustine Beach/Palatka, and follow it 3 miles. Turn right onto the access road, and follow it to the end. You can park to the right of the trailhead, which will be directly to your left.

To reach the southern trailhead in Spuds from I-95, take Exit 311. Head south on FL 207 toward St. Augustine Beach/Palatka, and follow it 9.2 miles. The intersection at FL 207 and County Road 207 is 0.3 mile south of CR 13 and less than 0.1 mile north of Nixon Lane.

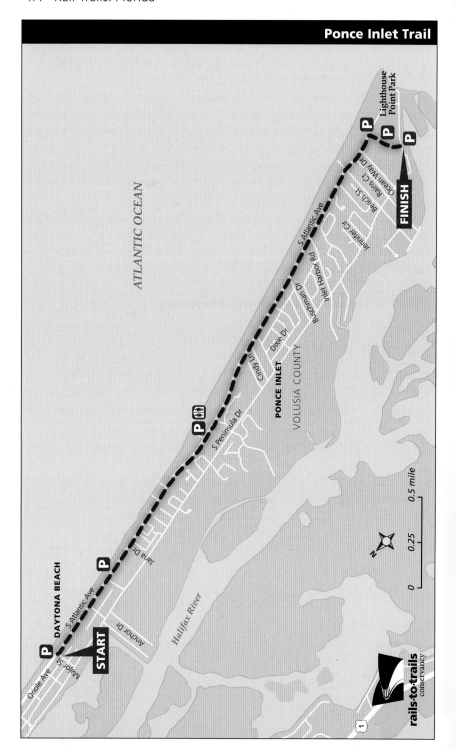

The Ponce Inlet, lighthouse, and trail are named after the Spanish conquistador Juan Ponce de León, who is credited with leading the first European expedition to Florida. The trail stretches along the ocean shore through most of the Ponce Inlet, ending at Lighthouse Point Park. While there is no major signage for the trail at the north endpoint at Major Street, a sign next to the trailhead reads WELCOME TO PONCE INLET. Here, you will also find parking.

The majority of the trail encompasses enlarged cement sidewalks that cross driveways and small intersections of different neighborhoods and gated communities. The town itself has the feel of a polished beach town on the Central Florida coast; it seems to embrace

The Ponce Inlet Trail is known for its spectacular views of the surrounding neighborhoods and coastal waterways.

Location
Volusia

Endpoints
Major St. and S. Atlantic Ave. (Port Orange) to S. Peninsula Drive and Lighthouse Drive (Ponce Inlet)

Mileage
3.5

Type
Greenway/Non-Rail-Trail

Roughness Index
1

Surface
Concrete

the wildlife of the area, with lots of pelicans and pelican-themed statues and signs. The Marine Science Center is also located at the south end of the trail in Lighthouse Point Park.

A unique and practical feature of this trail is the use of flags to safely cross the street. At an intersection, walkers take a provided yellow flag from the flag holder attached to a sign on one side of the street and leave it in the flag holder on the opposite side after they cross. Because of the number of crossings on the trail, this is a great feature for securing a safe active-transportation environment.

Coasting along past potted palm trees and nicely manicured lawns, you'll notice that this trail has few hills or rough spots. At times, you can hear and see the ocean to your left. The farther down the trail you head, the more you become aware that you're following an inlet. Eventually, the trail turns into a small sidewalk and ends at a pleasant playground near the Halifax River. The lighthouse itself—the tallest in Florida—is to the right (around the corner) of the trail's terminus. You may want to try climbing to the top of the lighthouse for a spectacular view of the surrounding coastal waterways and neighborhoods.

Nearby Lighthouse Point Park contains some great green space and historic markers, and lots of small walking routes through and along watery areas with plenty of wildlife.

CONTACT: volusia.org/services/community-services/parks-recreation-and-culture

DIRECTIONS

To reach the Major St. trailhead from I-95, take Exit 256 for US 1. Head northeast on FL 421 E./ Dunlawton Ave. Drive 5.1 miles. Turn right onto S. Atlantic Ave. After 2.2 miles, look for parking on the right along the road (just past the Major St. intersection).

To reach the trailhead at Lighthouse Point Park, follow the directions above to S. Atlantic Ave. Drive 5.1 miles, and turn right onto Lighthouse Drive. You'll find plenty of parking along the short stretch toward S. Peninsula Drive (where the trail begins), as well as at the Marine Science Center to your right on Lighthouse Drive.

The busy Ream Wilson Clearwater Trail serves as an attractive destination and transportation route for Clearwater residents and visitors. It meanders through residential neighborhoods, public parkland, and a large number of municipal sports complexes, including the Philadelphia Phillies' spring training camp.

The pleasant 4.4-mile route features Florida's offerings in those spaces in between—where nature and suburbs meet—and trail users will appreciate the residential communities, public parks with endless recreation opportunities, and up-close access to coastal Florida's ecosystems. Starting at the western trailhead near Clearwater's Long Center, the trail heads east through a series of parks and public rights-of-way, with great access to tennis courts, ball fields, disc golf courses, and more. The western

The Ream Wilson—where nature and the suburbs meet.

Location
Pinellas

Endpoints
Old Coachman Road near Farrier Trail (Clearwater) to Veterans Memorial Lane and S. Bayshore Blvd. (Safety Harbor)

Mileage
4.4

Type
Greenway/Non-Rail-Trail

Roughness Index
1

Surface
Asphalt, Concrete

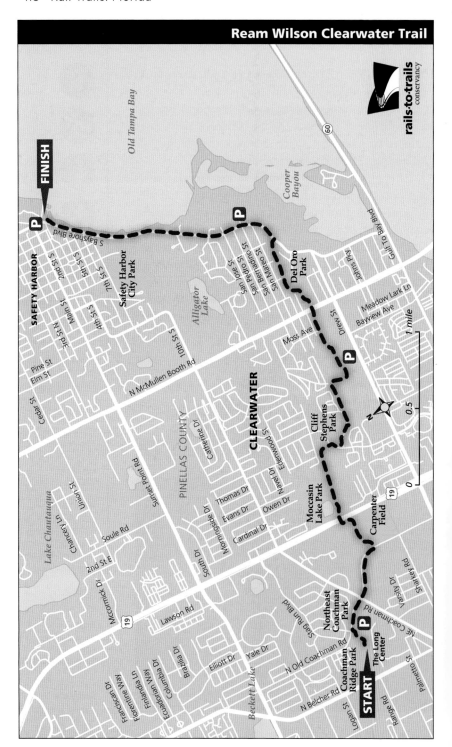

Ream Wilson Clearwater Trail

FINISH

Old Tampa Bay

Cooper Bayou

60

Gulf to Bay Blvd

S Bayshore Blvd

SAFETY HARBOR

2nd St S
3rd St N
Main St
5th St S
4th St S
7th St S

Safety Harbor City Park

San Jose St
San Pedro St
San Bernadino St
San Mateo St

Del Oro Park

Johns Pky

Meadow Lark Ln
Bayview Ave

Drew St

Moss Ave

Pine St
Elm St

Alligator Lake

10th St S

N McMullen Booth Rd

CLEARWATER

Cedar St

Catherine Dr

Cliff Stephens Park

Edenwood St

1 mile

0.5

N

PINELLAS COUNTY

Lake Chantauqua

Union St

Chancey Ln

Sunset Point Rd

Catherine Dr

Thomas Dr

Evans Dr

Cardinal Dr

Navel Dr

Owen Dr

Moccasin Lake Park

0

Soule Rd

Morningside Dr

South Dr

Carpenter Field

19

McCormick Dr

2nd St E

19

Lawson Rd

Franciscan Dr
Florentine Way
Finlandia Ln
Ecuadorian Dr
Columbia Dr

Brazilia Dr

Elliott Dr

Yale Dr

Stag Run Blvd

N Old Coachman Rd

Northeast Coachman Park

Coachman Ridge Park

NE Coachman Rd

Varsity Dr

Starkey Rd

Beckett Lake

Logan St

N Belcher Rd

The Long Center

START

Range Rd

Palmetto St

rails·to·trails
conservancy

portion of the trail intersects Coachman Ridge Park with handsome oak trees surrounding well-kept ball courts with parking and drinking water.

Let the migrating birds and local waterfowl provide the sound track as you proceed east under impressive live oaks, which provide a shady respite from the Florida sun as the trail crisscrosses small streams and passes through quiet neighborhoods and well-used parks. Keep an eye and ear out for some impressive Florida birds, and even a reptile or two, as this trail blends the perfect balance of urban connectivity with the coastal Florida ecosystem.

After you pass under US 19, you may have a close encounter with a freight train, as the trail parallels an active CSX line. You'll soon reach Cliff Stephens Park, which is sure to keep you entertained with its abundant recreational and people-watching opportunities. From here, the trail continues toward Tampa Bay, past a nice series of waterfront parks with parking, drinking fountains, walking paths, public exercise equipment, and waterfront views. After this section, the trail turns left and runs adjacent to Bayshore Boulevard, where you can enjoy periodic views of, and fishing access to, Cooper Bayou as it opens into Tampa Bay.

CONTACT: clearwater-fl.com/gov/depts/parksrec/bikeways/east_west.asp

DIRECTIONS

The western end of the trail can be accessed at Clearwater's Long Center. From I-275, take Exit 39 and follow signs for FL 60. Head west on FL 60, and drive 12.2 miles. Turn right onto S. Belcher Road, and in 1.3 miles turn right just past the train tracks into the Long Center complex (you'll be routed around several sports fields to the parking lot). The trail begins in the back of the complex.

Parking is also available at the western end of the trail in Coachman Ridge Park (1400 Coachman Road), adjacent to the Long Center. From I-275, take Exit 39 and follow signs for FL 60. Head west on FL 60, and drive 11.5 miles. Turn right onto Old Coachman Road. In 1.5 miles turn left into the parking lot for the park.

To reach the eastern trailhead at Veterans Memorial Lane from I-275, take Exit 39 and follow signs for FL 60. Head west on FL 60, and drive 9.7 miles. Turn right onto Bayshore Blvd. In 2.4 miles turn right onto Veterans Memorial Lane. Parking is available on the right.

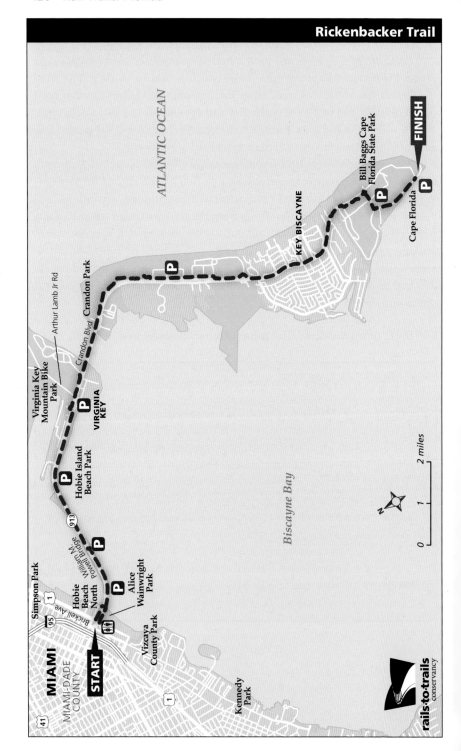

Rickenbacker Trail

Rickenbacker Trail begins in southern Miami and continues south along the Rickenbacker Causeway/ Crandon Boulevard about 8.5 miles, traversing the length of Key Biscayne. Along this popular route, you'll have beautiful views of Biscayne Bay, beaches, and palm trees. There is no charge for pedestrians or cyclists entering the Key, and there are popular add-on routes that many local cyclists incorporate to extend their total distance. Enhancements have been made to the trail in recent years, including a new toll plaza entranceway for bicycles, green-painted bike lanes, and improved intersections.

The trail's route parallels open water and weaves through a coastal hammock. A couple of sections of trail also briefly merge onto highway bridges to cross Biscayne

Perfect for bike users, the Rickenbacker Trail provides beautiful palm tree views of Biscayne Bay.

Location
Miami-Dade

Endpoints
Alice Wainwright Park at FL 913/Rickenbacker Causeway and Brickell Ave. (Miami) to Bill Baggs Cape Florida State Park at Cape Florida Park Blvd. at Biscayne Bay (Key Biscayne)

Mileage
8.5

Type
Greenway/Non-Rail-Trail

Roughness Index
1

Surface
Asphalt, Concrete

Bay; these bridges provide wide bike lanes. Pedestrians and runners are separated on the causeway in their own protected lanes.

Begin your journey at Alice Wainwright Park, which is open sunrise–sunset. Restrooms and on-street parking are available here. You can also access another endpoint at Southwest 26th Road and Brickell Avenue, which cuts to the right onto a sidewalk that extends underneath Rickenbacker Causeway and then back up to the trail, allowing you to avoid crossing at the busy intersection of the causeway and Brickell Avenue.

After crossing the water on the causeway, you'll reach Hobie Beach North (located on a small island) and then the William M. Powell Bridge, which is popular with the Miami cycling community. In addition to providing views of the water, the short, single-span structure is the closest thing to a hill in South Florida; don't be afraid to use your bike gears for assistance.

Reentering land, you will pass Hobie Island Beach Park, which provides excellent access to Biscayne Bay. Around the park are numerous places to rent all types of watercraft, as well as an aquarium, a restaurant, and other attractions. Continuing south along Crandon Boulevard, you'll come to Bill Baggs Cape Florida State Park (there is a fee for trail users), which has a lighthouse, restaurants with good views of the water, restrooms, and shower facilities. Inside the park, the trail cuts right and then left toward the southern terminus at Cape Florida; you can also head through the state park via an add-on bike lane south of Crandon Park.

If you decide to take the trail back to its northern terminus, you may want to add Arthur Lamb Jr. Road (on Virginia Key between Miami and Key Biscayne) to your route. The road leads east a short distance to one of the few mountain bike areas in Miami—Virginia Key Mountain Bike Park—which accommodates many different riding levels.

CONTACT: www.miamidade.gov/parksmasterplan/library/rick.pdf

DIRECTIONS

To reach Alice Wainwright Park (2845 Brickell Ave.) from I-95 S., take Exit 1A toward Key Biscayne/Rickenbacker Causeway. Turn left onto S.W. 26th Road, and immediately turn right onto S. Miami Ave. After 0.4 mile, turn left onto S.E. 32nd Road, and then continue on Brickell Ave. The park will be to your right in 0.4 mile. On-street parking is available in the residential area around the park.

To reach the southern trailhead from I-95 S., take Exit 1A toward Key Biscayne/ Rickenbacker Causeway. Turn left onto S.W. 26th Road, and continue on FL 913 S./ Rickenbacker Causeway (partial toll road); drive 5.8 miles. Continue on Crandon Blvd. 2.2 miles, and continue on Cape Florida Park Blvd. In another 0.5 mile, the road dead-ends into the trailhead parking lot. The trail entrance is just ahead at the end of Cape Florida Park Blvd. Note that there are many access points and parking areas along the Rickenbacker Causeway. Crandon Park (6746 Crandon Blvd.) has numerous amenities for trail users, and parking is available for a fee.

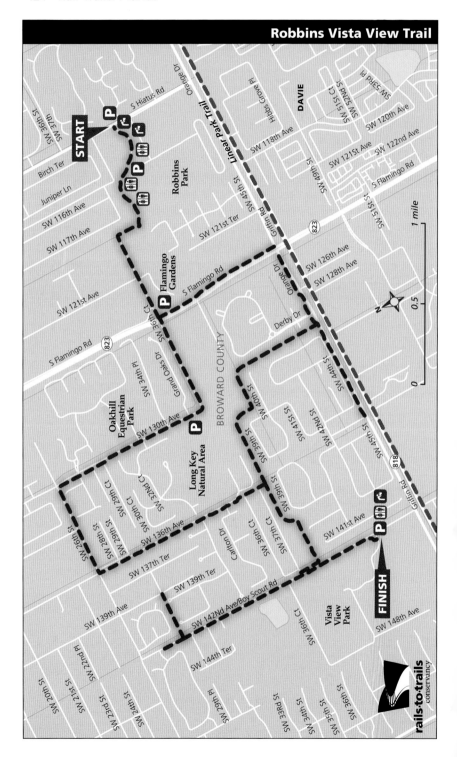

Robbins Vista View Trail

Robbins Vista View Trail is actually a network of greenway trails that runs through Broward County. The trails meander mostly through residential areas, with some along roads. Starting at Robbins Park on the eastern side, the trail passes plenty of restrooms and drinking fountains, after which it transports you into a lush wooded area where you'll have the opportunity to see lizards and tortoises roaming about.

You'll pass Flamingo Gardens—a botanical collection and Everglades wildlife sanctuary—on the corner of FL 823 and Southwest 36th Court. The site provides educational opportunities for children and adults, with exhibits including birds of prey, flamingos, panthers, bobcats, and black bears. Continuing along the trail to your right, you'll eventually pass the 165-acre Long Key Natural Area, which contains one of the largest remaining stands of upland hardwood forest in Broward County. A series of trail segments on the south side of the network will take you around residential areas.

Pleasant parks and residential areas can be found along the meandering route of the Robbins Vista View Trail.

Location
Broward

Endpoints
Robbins Park at S. Hiatus Road and 40th Place to S.W. 26th St. to Vista View Park at Boy Scout Road near Orange Drive (Davie)

Mileage
9

Type
Greenway/Non-Rail-Trail

Roughness Index
1

Surface
Asphalt, Concrete

At the western end of the trail network, you'll find Vista View Park, which offers recreational accommodations for a range of outdoor activities, including camping and fishing. The park also has an airfield for model planes and a paragliding club for the more adventurous. You might have a picnic at one of the park's many picnic shelters, which have tables, grills, and electric outlets.

If you still have energy left after your trip on the Robbins Vista View Trail, check out the 8.7-mile Linear Park Trail just south of the Vista View, or head north to the 7.5-mile New River Greenway.

CONTACT: www.davie-fl.gov/gen/daviefl_publicwrks/trails/recrobbins

DIRECTIONS

To access the eastern trailhead at Robbins Park from I-595 E., take Exits 3 and 4, and follow signs for FL 84 and Hiatus Road. Merge onto FL 84 E., and in 0.6 mile turn right onto S.W. 112th Ave./S. Hiatus Road. In 2.7 miles turn right into the park. The trailhead is immediately to your right, and parking is directly ahead. From I-595 W., take Exits 3 and 2, and follow signs for FL 84 and Hiatus Road. Merge onto FL 84 W., and take the Hiatus Road ramp. In 0.4 mile turn left onto S.W. 112th Ave./S. Hiatus Road. In 2.6 miles turn right into the park. The trailhead is immediately to your right, and parking is directly ahead.

To access the western trailhead at Vista View Park from I-595 E., take Exit 2 toward FL 823/Flamingo Road. Merge onto FL 84 E., and immediately turn right onto S. Flamingo Road. After 3.4 miles, turn right onto S.W. 45th St./Orange Drive, and go 1.5 miles. Turn right onto S.W. 142nd Ave./Boy Scout Road and then left into the park. Curve right and then left on the access road, and then turn right into the parking lot access (and left into the lot). From I-595 W., take Exits 3 and 2, and follow signs for FL 84 and Hiatus Road. Merge onto FL 84 W, and drive 1.5 miles. Turn left onto S. Flamingo Road. After 3.5 miles, turn right onto S.W. 45th St./Orange Drive, and go 1.5 miles. Turn right onto S.W. 142nd Ave./Boy Scout Road, and in 0.2 mile turn left into the park. Curve right and then left on the access road, and then turn right into the parking lot access (and left into the lot).

The treasures of Sanibel Island, off Florida's southwest coast, are easily accessible by a connected network of paved, shared-use pathways. Although many of the trails parallel the island's main streets, they are separated from traffic by grassy medians and connect visitors to Sanibel's numerous attractions.

The island is connected to the mainland by the Sanibel Causeway on its northeastern shore. Soon after arriving on the island, you'll see the brightly colored chamber of commerce and visitor center on your right; be sure to stop here for maps and trip-planning information.

The island's main thoroughfare is Periwinkle Way, and the pathway follows the south side of the roadway, offering convenient access to restaurants and shops. If you

Location
Lee

Endpoints
Sanibel Lighthouse on Periwinkle Way at the Gulf of Mexico (Sanibel) to Turner Beach on Captiva Drive at Blind Pass (Captiva)

Mileage
24

Type
Greenway/Non-Rail-Trail

Roughness Index
1

Surface
Asphalt

The Sanibel Island Lighthouse, located at the eastern terminus of the trail

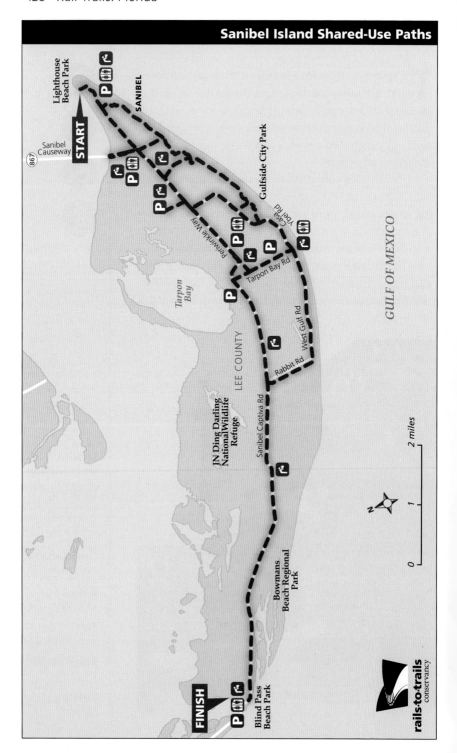

Sanibel Island Shared-Use Paths

head east along Periwinkle Way, you'll be rewarded with a visit to the Sanibel Lighthouse, the island's most famous landmark.

If you head west, Periwinkle Way ends at a T-juncture with Tarpon Bay Road. Take a right and follow the path north until you can take a left onto the pathway paralleling Sanibel Captiva Road. This will take you past the Bailey-Matthews Shell Museum, featuring exhibits on shell art, mollusk habitats, fossils, and native Florida varieties. Continue west down Sanibel Captiva Road until you see the entrance to the J. N. Ding Darling National Wildlife Refuge at Wildlife Drive on your right. The park protects one of the country's largest undeveloped mangrove ecosystems; explore its 5,200 acres on foot, by bike, or even via kayak.

You can continue along Sanibel Captiva Road all the way across the island to Blind Pass Beach Park on its western shore, or to Turner Beach, which is located across the water a short distance on Captiva Island.

If you want to see the island's popular southern shoreline, take a left from Sanibel Captiva Road onto Rabbit Road just before you get to the wildlife refuge. Part of the route that parallels Rabbit Road is along a wooded canal; look for alligators, herons, and the marsh rabbits for which the road is named. After about a mile, you'll reach West Gulf Drive. Turn left to continue on the pathway east to see beautiful waterfront estates and hotels. When the road makes a northern upswing, it becomes Casa Ybel Road, which will take you back up to Periwinkle Way.

CONTACT: mysanibel.com/departments/recreation2/outdoor-recreation

DIRECTIONS

To reach Sanibel Island Visitor Center: From I-75, take Exit 131 toward Southwest Florida International Airport/Cape Coral. Head west on Daniels Pkwy., and continue 7.32 miles (after 4.5 miles, the road becomes Cypress Lake Drive). Turn left onto FL 867/McGregor Blvd. Continue 2.8 miles, and turn right to stay on McGregor Blvd. Continue another 2.7 miles, and then turn right again to stay on McGregor Blvd. After 1.7 miles, continue onto the Sanibel Causeway (partial toll road) 3.3 miles to Sanibel Island. Once you reach the island, the causeway turns into Causeway Blvd. After 0.3 mile, look for the brightly colored visitor center (1159 Causeway Blvd.) on your right. Parking is available here and at all of the public beaches that dot the island.

To reach the eastern trailhead at Lighthouse Beach Park, follow the directions above to take the Sanibel Causeway to Causeway Blvd. After 0.4 mile, turn left onto Periwinkle Way. After 1.5 miles, continue straight into the parking lot.

To reach the parking lot at Blind Pass Beach Park, follow the directions above to take the Sanibel Causeway to Causeway Blvd. After 0.4 mile, turn right onto Periwinkle Way, and continue 2.5 miles; then make a slight right onto Palm Ridge Road. After 0.4 mile, continue on Sanibel Captiva Road 7.2 miles. Turn left into the parking lot.

To reach the Turner Beach trailhead and parking, follow the directions to Blind Pass Beach Park, and continue on Sanibel Captiva Road over the Blind Pass Bridge. Parking is available to your left at the end of the bridge.

The 14-mile Seminole Wekiva Trail is one of the most popular trails in Seminole County, offering a variety of experiences, landscapes, and amenities for trail users of all ages. The well-marked pathway follows the former route of the Orange Belt Railway, established in 1885, and information kiosks along the trail offer small lessons to trail users curious about the region's railroad history.

Starting at the northwest trailhead, you'll pass through quiet residential neighborhoods and a Spanish moss–draped tree canopy that provides welcome shade from the Florida sun. Just after the Seminole Soccer Club Complex and Orlando City youth soccer club, stop at the pond overlook to enjoy views of frogs jumping from lily pad to lily pad as birds patrol the water's edge.

The middle section of trail offers a more suburban feel with shopping centers and plenty of restaurants. You'll pass business complexes and modern office buildings,

Hundreds of colorful paintings by artist Jeff Sonksen decorate the southern portion of the Seminole Wekiva Trail.

Location
Seminole

Endpoints
Markham Road near County Road 46A in the Wekiva River Protection Area (Lake Mary) to FL 436 near Laurel St. (Altamonte Springs)

Mileage
14

Type
Rail-Trail

Roughness Index
1

Surface
Asphalt

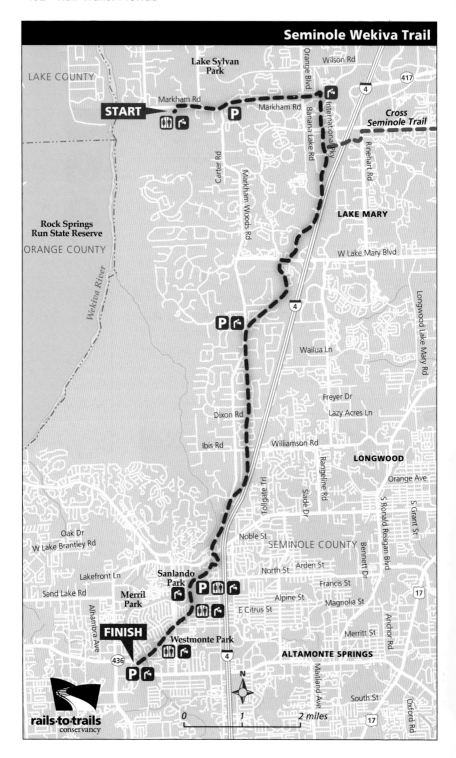

eventually arriving at a pedestrian bridge over I-4. This spur connects you to the Cross Seminole Trail.

The southern part of the route mirrors the peaceful scenery of the northern section, with the added benefit of art displayed along the trail. Through a project titled *Paint the Trail,* artist Jeff Sonksen has installed hundreds of paintings with themes ranging from current events to movies and music.

After exploring the Seminole Wekiva Trail, check out the nearby 22.8-mile Cross Seminole Trail (see page 35) that extends east and south to Oviedo.

CONTACT: seminolecountyfl.gov

DIRECTIONS

To access the northern trailhead from I-4, take Exit 98 toward Lake Mary/Heathrow. Head west on W. Lake Mary Blvd. Continue 1.3 miles, and turn right onto Markham Woods Road. After 2.5 miles, turn left onto Markham Road, and go 0.8 mile. Turn left into the trailhead.

To access the southern endpoint from I-4, take Exit 92 for FL 436 toward Altamonte Springs/Apopka. Head west on FL 436, and go 1.7 miles. Turn right into the access road, the next street past Riverbend Drive (if you pass San Sebastian Prado, you've gone too far), and turn left into the trailhead parking lot.

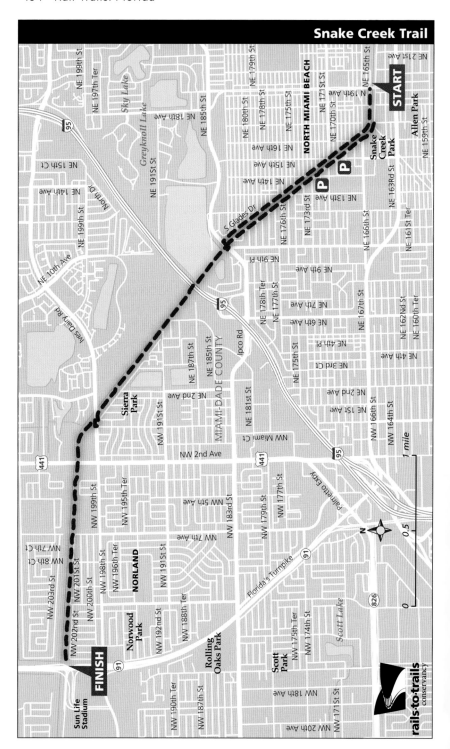

Snake Creek Trail

Snake Creek Trail is named for its curvy route, which runs along the water of the Snake Creek Canal. The northern section is nestled along the neighborhoods of Norland, northwest of the North Miami Beach area.

The southeastern portion—a good starting point— is split, with one segment starting at North Glades Drive and Northeast 19th Avenue (north of the canal), and the other segment starting at South Glades Drive and Miami Drive (south of the canal, near Snake Creek Park). The segments follow the canal north to 185th Street, with a few street crossings along the way. An emphasis on health is prevalent; as you begin your journey, you'll see the words "Heart, Health, Walk" painted on the trail, as well as a red bike rack in the shape of a heart. As you progress northwest on both sides, you'll pass workout stations and exercise machines, benches, trashcans, and an inviting

Trail amenities along the Snake Creek Trail include an impressive variety of fitness stations.

Location
Miami-Dade

Endpoints
S. Glades Drive and Miami Drive or N. Glades Drive and N.E. 19th Ave. (North Miami Beach) to N.W. 202nd St. and N.W. 15th Ave. (Norland)

Mileage
6.5

Type
Greenway/Non-Rail-Trail

Roughness Index
1

Surface
Asphalt

rubber-animal play spot for children. This stretch feels like an extended linear park along water.

Wildlife is also prevalent; be sure to keep an eye out for waterfowl and other birds, fish, and large iguanas. The lizards, which are particularly common along the trail, can be seen in the lush grass or on the trail soaking up the sun. The trail is also speckled with backyards boasting fruit trees and flowers, creating a pleasant environment.

Most of the trail runs through easy, open areas with few road crossings. About midway along your journey, you'll approach a low overpass bridge; at this section, which is unsafe for bicycle riding, bicyclists should walk their bikes. There are steps on the western side of the overpass. While the canal route is generally flat with few sharp turns, there is one big curve to the left as you head north just after Northwest 199th Street, after which you find yourself facing almost directly west. In the distance, you'll see Sun Life Stadium, home of the Miami Dolphins.

The last stretch of the trail is open and calm, running along the back side of neighboring houses. The trail ends at a cul-de-sac, which provides a clear view of Sun Life Stadium just across the toll road (Florida's Turnpike).

CONTACT: www.miamidade.gov/parksmasterplan/library/snake.pdf

DIRECTIONS

To reach the S. Glades Drive trailhead from I-95, take Exit 14 for FL 860 toward Miami Gardens Drive. Turn left onto FL 860 E./Miami Gardens Drive/N.E. 183rd St. After 1.3 miles, turn right onto N.E. 15th Ave., and continue 1.1 miles. Turn left onto N.E. 167th St. The trailhead will be directly in front of you along the creek, and there is ample parking on either side of the street.

To reach the N. Glades Drive trailhead from I-95, take Exit 14 for FL 860 toward Miami Gardens Drive. Turn left onto FL 860 E./Miami Gardens Drive/N.E. 183rd St. After 1.3 miles, turn right onto N.E. 15th Ave., and continue 0.8 mile. Turn left onto N.E. 171st St., and drive 0.4 mile. Turn right onto N.E. 18th Ave. The trailhead is 0.3 mile ahead at the intersection with N. Glades Drive and the canal.

To reach the Norland trailhead from I-95, take Exit 12A or 12 for US 441/FL 9/FL 826. Follow signs for FL 826, and merge onto FL 826. Continue on Florida's Turnpike/FL 91 (toll road), and in 1.8 miles take Exit 2X toward N.W. 199th St./Stadium. Turn left onto N.W. 199th St. After 0.4 mile, turn left onto N.W. 14th Court, and go 0.2 mile. Turn left onto N.W. 202nd St. This is a residential area with limited on-street parking.

South Lake Trail (also known as Lake Minneola Scenic Trail) contains some of Central Florida's most spectacular views and neighborhoods. Nowhere in this region will you find more hills, lakes, and wide-open vistas than along this 13-mile paved trail. The trail is also part of a larger network called the Coast-to-Coast Connector, which will stretch across Central Florida from St. Petersburg to Cape Canaveral.

This trail starts where the West Orange Trail ends at the Killarney Station trailhead on Old County Road 50. From there, it meanders through hilltops and wooded valleys to Hancock Road, where you can test your hill-climbing skills and ride southeast to Lake-Sumter State College, or continue west to the shore of Lake Minneola in Clermont. After a few miles, you'll come to a trail shelter with benches and a plaque honoring a fallen cyclist who frequented the

On clear days, the South Lake and Lake Minneola Scenic Trail provides views of the entire region.

Location
Lake

Endpoints
West Orange Trail at Killarney Station at Old County Road 50/FL 438 and Lake Blvd. (Oakland) to CR 565A and Silver Eagle Road (Clermont)

Mileage
13

Type
Rail-Trail

Roughness Index
1

Surface
Asphalt

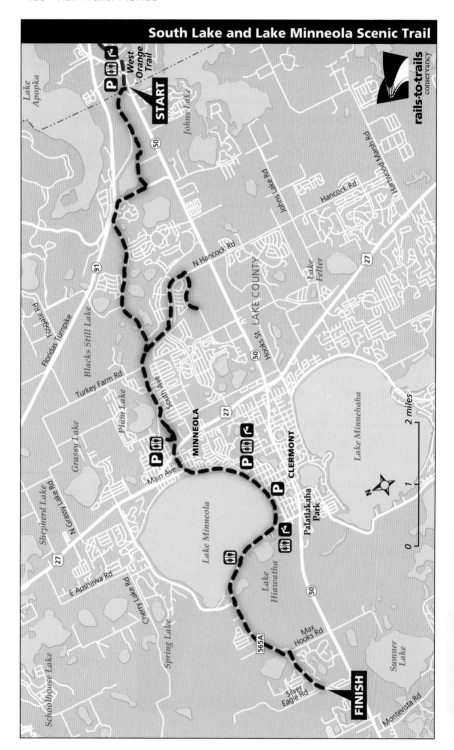

trail. On a clear day, you'll have wonderful views of the entire region, from glimmering lakes to the Orlando skyline. Along this part of the route, you'll find many stores, including a bike shop, and several downtown areas close to the trail. Streetlamps allow for safe nighttime travel through this commonly used section.

As it skirts the southern shore, the trail offers beautiful views of the lake, as well as a beach and swimming area. Clermont Public Beach boasts cool water and trailside amenities such as restrooms, picnic tables, and parking. Along the beach, you'll find new playgrounds, including one with musical instruments for children. Any of the side streets leading away from the lake will take you to shops and restaurants in downtown Clermont. In 2015, the trail was extended farther west of Clermont to Silver Eagle Road (ending across from the Green Valley Golf Club). The new segment includes two new pedestrian bridges and fishing areas.

CONTACT: lakecountyfl.gov/departments/public_resources/parks

DIRECTIONS

To reach the Killarney Station trailhead from I-4, take Exit 77 toward Ocala (partial toll road), and merge onto Florida's Turnpike (toll road), heading northwest. Drive 12.6 miles, and take Exit 272 toward Clermont. Merge onto FL 50 W./W. Colonial Drive. Follow FL 50 W. 1.4 miles, and turn right onto Lake Blvd. After 0.2 mile, turn right onto FL 438 S./Old County Road 50 E. Immediately turn right into the trailhead.

To reach the Clermont trailhead from I-4, follow directions above to FL 50 W., and drive 11.4 miles. Turn right (north) onto CR 565A, and follow the road 0.6 mile. Turn left onto Silver Eagle Road. Parking is immediately to your left; the trailhead is on the right, directly across the road.

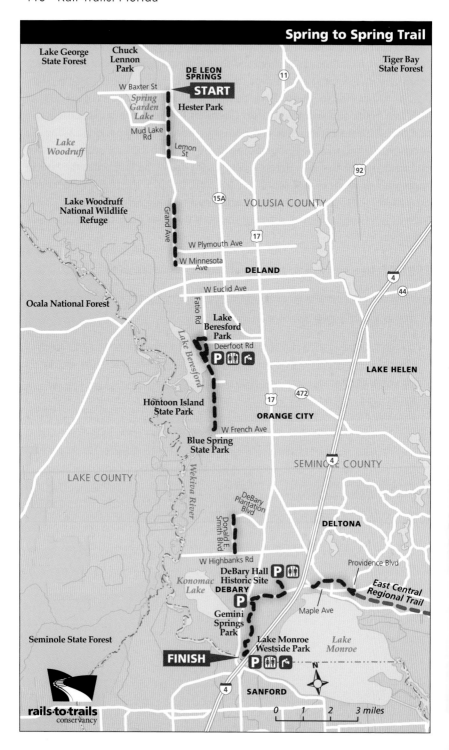

Spring to Spring Trail

Lake George State Forest

Chuck Lennon Park

DE LEON SPRINGS

START

W Baxter St

Spring Garden Lake

Hester Park

Mud Lake Rd

Lemon St

Tiger Bay State Forest

11

Lake Woodruff

Lake Woodruff National Wildlife Refuge

92

Grand Ave

15A

VOLUSIA COUNTY

W Plymouth Ave

17

W Minnesota Ave

DELAND

Ocala National Forest

W Euclid Ave

4

44

Fatio Rd

Lake Beresford Park

Deerfoot Rd

Lake Beresford

LAKE HELEN

Hontoon Island State Park

17   472

ORANGE CITY

W French Ave

Blue Spring State Park

Wekiva River

SEMINOLE COUNTY

4

LAKE COUNTY

DeBary Plantation Blvd

DELTONA

Donald E. Smith Blvd

W Highbanks Rd

Providence Blvd

DeBary Hall Historic Site

Konomac Lake

DEBARY

East Central Regional Trail

Gemini Springs Park

Maple Ave

Lake Monroe

FINISH

Lake Monroe Westside Park

Seminole State Forest

N

rails·to·trails conservancy

4   **SANFORD**

0   1   2   3 miles

Northernmost Section

Grand Ave. and W. Baxter St. (De Leon Springs) to Grand Ave. at Grandwood Estates (DeLand): 4.3 miles

The northern section of the Spring to Spring Trail network is hidden along Grand Avenue in the town of De Leon Springs. The pathway begins as a sidewalk-like surface on the right side of the road (heading south); however, when it switches to the other side of the road at Katrina Street, you'll start to get the sense that you're on a trail. Not long after the switch, you'll come to Mud Lake Road; if you turn right here, you'll head toward the entrance to a

Location
Volusia

Endpoints
Grand Ave. and W. Baxter St. (De Leon Springs) to Grand Ave., 0.5 mile south of W. Plymouth Ave. (DeLand); Lake Beresford Park at Deerfoot Road and Fatio Road (DeLand) to Blue Spring State Park at W. French Ave. and Becker Blvd. (Orange City); Donald E. Smith Blvd. and DeBary Plantation Blvd. to Donald E. Smith Blvd. and W. Highbanks Road (DeLand); DeBary Ave. and Providence Blvd. (Deltona) to Lake Monroe Park at Old DeLand Road near US 17 (DeBary)

Mileage
17

Type
Greenway/Non-Rail-Trail

Roughness Index
1

Surface
Asphalt

A beautiful canopy of Spanish moss awaits trail users on the Spring to Spring Trail.

2,300-acre wildlife refuge at Lake Woodruff. The refuge is home to a variety of land and water fauna, including seven endangered species and more than 230 species of birds.

As you continue down the trail, you'll eventually come to a 1.6-mile, on-road section of trail. Luckily, this section is residential, and car traffic is minimal. Heading toward DeLand back on the trail, the landscape opens up a bit to some farms and wetlands, ending where the road makes its first sharp left onto West Minnesota Avenue (at West Minnesota Estates).

DIRECTIONS

To reach the northern trailhead from I-4, take Exit 118A for FL 44 toward New Smyrna Beach/ DeLand Historic District. Follow signs for FL 44 W./DeLand Historic District, and head west on FL 44 W./E. New York Ave. After 4.4 miles, turn right (north) onto N. Amelia Ave. Go 1.8 miles, and turn left onto E. International Speedway Blvd. In 0.2 mile turn right onto US 17 N./N. Woodland Blvd., and go 5.6 miles. Turn left onto Wheeler St. and immediately turn right onto Grand Ave. The trailhead is to your left, near where Grand Ave. meets W. Baxter St. Note: The northern section of trail is mostly residential, and there is no formal parking adjacent to the trail.

Lake Beresford Park at Deerfoot Road and Fatio Road (DeLand) to Blue Spring State Park at W. French Ave. and Becker Blvd. (Orange City): 5.4 miles

The trail picks up on the southwestern outskirts of DeLand, the seat of Volusia County and home to Stetson University. This segment begins at Lake Beresford Park, not far from the banks of the 2-mile-long lake, whose calm waters are a favorite of rowers. Parking, water, and restrooms are available near the trailhead.

The trail travels south along Blue Spring State Park for just over 3 miles, through an environment lush with tropical hammocks (forests) and magnolia trees, and ends near the park entrance. The park is a designated manatee refuge, and trail users can learn more about this endangered animal through ranger programs and view them from an observation platform during the winter, when manatees gather in the warm waters of the spring. Swimmers, snorkelers, and even scuba divers can also enjoy the spring. Restrooms, parking, and other amenities are available for paid park visitors.

DIRECTIONS

To reach the trailhead at Lake Beresford Park from I-4, take Exit 116 toward Orange Camp Road. Head west on Orange Camp Road, which becomes McGregor Road, and drive 5 miles. Turn right onto Fatio Road, and in 0.5 mile turn left into the park.

To reach the trailhead at Blue Spring State Park, take I-4 to Exit 114 for FL 472 toward Deltona/DeLand. Head northwest on FL 472, and drive 3.2 miles. Merge onto US 17/US 92, heading south. Continue 1.7 miles, and turn right onto W. French Ave. In 2.1 miles, you'll reach the trailhead. Parking and other amenities are available for paid park visitors.

Lake Beresford Section

Donald E. Smith Blvd. and DeBary Plantation Blvd. to Donald E. Smith Blvd. and W. Highbanks Road (DeLand): 1.3 miles

A short 1.3-mile section of trail south of the main DeLand trail, located on Donald E. Smith Boulevard between DeBary Plantation Boulevard and West Highbanks Road, runs primarily through residential areas.

DIRECTIONS

Parking is not available along this stretch of trail.

Gemini Springs (DeBary Hall) Section

DeBary Ave. and Providence Blvd. (Deltona) to Lake Monroe Park at Old DeLand Road near US 17 (DeBary): 6 miles

One of the most lush and scenic portions of the trail traces the northwest shoreline of Lake Monroe.

Technically this section of trail begins at Providence Boulevard along DeBary Avenue; additionally, a very short spur at DeBary Avenue and Jacob Brock Avenue (almost at the endpoint) connects to the western endpoint of the East Central Regional Rail Trail. However, a little less than 2 miles after beginning your journey at this endpoint, you'll reach Welcome Center Drive; here, the trail stops, resulting in a 1-mile gap until you reach Mansion Boulevard. Therefore, the Providence endpoint is not recommended as a starting point for those who wish to avoid on-road bicycling or walking. Additionally, there is no trail parking at this endpoint.

If you turn right onto Mansion Boulevard, you'll quickly dead-end at the DeBary Hall Historic Site (210 Sunrise Blvd.), an 8,000-square-foot estate that offers exhibits, multimedia programs, and guided tours; here, you can learn about the history of the St. Johns River region and the people that worked in the house and on the grounds during the late 1800s and early 1900s. This is also where the next section of trail begins and is the best place to begin your journey.

On the trail, you'll make your way through a lovely canopy-covered area rife with Spanish moss and palm wetlands on either side. Eventually, you'll reach a park entrance road crossing; notice the fighter jet memorial just across the main road.

The trail parallels the roadway west almost 2 miles to Gemini Springs Park, a picturesque 210-acre green space. You might stop for a picnic or take a stroll on one of its various nature trails. As you wind through Gemini Springs, the trail drops south a couple of miles to Lake Monroe Park, where it ends. At this terminus, you can take in some of the lake wildlife and access the water from the park's boat ramps and fishing docks.

DIRECTIONS

There is no trail parking at the Providence Blvd. endpoint.

To reach the DeBary trailhead at the DeBary Hall Historic Site from I-4, take Exit 108 toward Deltona/DeBary (0.4 mile). Head southwest on DeBary Ave. (if you are coming from the north, the road has already become Dirksen Drive). In 0.1 mile turn right onto Sunrise Blvd. After 0.6 mile, the road turns left; turn right into DeBary Hall. There are signs in front of DeBary Hall that direct you to visitor parking. The trailhead will be on your left at Mansion Blvd.

To reach the Lake Monroe Park trailhead from I-4, take Exit 104 for US 17/US 92 toward Sanford. Head north on US 17. In 0.8 mile turn right onto Old DeLand Road. Drive 0.5 mile, and turn right into the park. The trailhead is at the end of Old DeLand Road, on the left.

CONTACT: volusia.org/services/community-services/parks-recreation-and-culture

St. George Island Bike Path is a 6.3-mile trail offering a pleasant ocean-view-filled journey through sand dunes (you'll see sea oats and plenty of pine trees) and scrub habitat. During the summer, you may want to get your walk or ride in early to avoid the heat, and be sure to bring sunblock, as there is little shade along the trail. The trail mainly parallels Gulf Beach Drive, but the trip can be extended by visiting Dr. Julian G. Bruce St. George Island State Park, which stretches north along the remaining length of the island. You can also incorporate paved sections of Gorrie Drive, which parallels the trail.

A good starting point is the St. George Island State Park Visitor Center, located in the middle of the island. Here, you'll find free parking, restrooms, and the reconstructed Cape St. George Lighthouse. Nearby, you'll find restaurants offering fresh local fish, as well as bait shops

The St. George Island State Park Visitor Center and reconstructed Cape St. George Lighthouse

Location
Franklin

Endpoints
W. Gulf Beach Drive and W. 12th St. (St. George Island) to E. Gulf Beach Drive at Dr. Julian G. Bruce St. George Island State Park (Eastpoint)

Mileage
6.3

Type
Greenway/Non-Rail-Trail

Roughness Index
1

Surface
Asphalt, Concrete

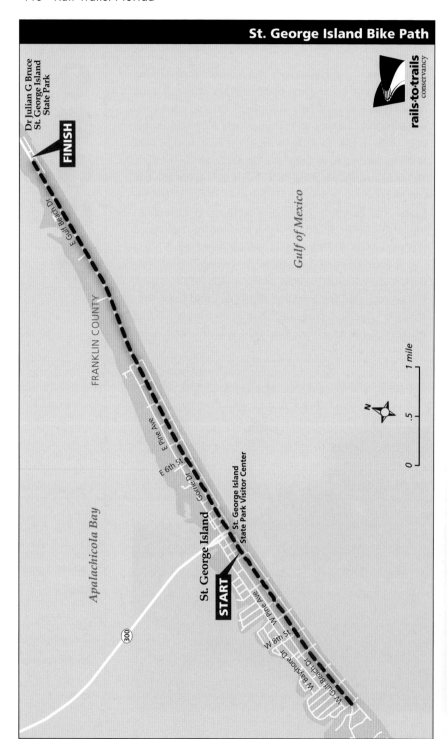

St. George Island Bike Path

for anglers. There are also plenty of options for overnight accommodations, ranging from hotel rooms to private rentals. It is worth noting that the island's beaches allow pets.

The Dr. Julian G. Bruce St. George Island State Park, on the eastern side of the trail, offers good beach access, ample parking, camping, and kayak rentals. If you are visiting between May and October, please be respectful of the loggerhead turtle. Mother turtles come ashore to lay their eggs, and at night, their babies scurry off to the sea.

CONTACT: seestgeorgeisland.com; floridastateparks.org/park/st-george-island

DIRECTIONS

To reach the St. George Island State Park Visitor Center from I-10, take Exit 120 for FL 77 toward Panama City. Head south on FL 77, and drive 43.1 miles. Turn left onto US 98/FL 30A/N.E. 15th St., and drive 60.1 miles, following signs for US 98. In Apalachicola turn right onto US 98/Big Bend Scenic Byway Coastal Trail, and go 6 miles. Turn right onto Island Drive/FL 300 in Eastpoint, and drive 5.6 miles. Turn right onto Gulf Beach Drive, and then take an immediate left onto W. Chili Blvd. Turn left into the visitor center parking lot. You can also access the trail from W. 12th St. and numerous public road crossings along the way. Park only at approved locations.

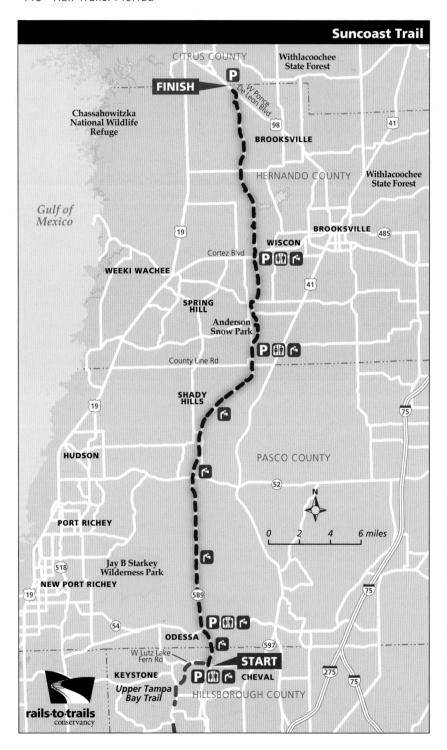

Suncoast Trail

Suncoast Trail offers 42 miles of paved riding pleasure, hugging the right-of-way of the Suncoast Parkway for its entire length.

A good starting point for your journey is the southern endpoint at the West Lutz Lake Fern Road trailhead in Keystone (technically part of the Upper Tampa Bay Trail). You'll quickly reach Pasco County, which provides many wayside stops with cold water and shade, a nod to the blistering Florida sun.

These water stops are not provided in Hernando County—your next destination along the route—so pack extra water accordingly. The first 2.5 miles are dotted with residential areas, after which you'll come to the first major road crossing at FL 54, where you'll find a significant retail establishment, as well as a trailhead with parking and water facilities. Four more miles of classic Southern

Rural, suburban, forest, and open scrub landscapes dominate the Suncoast Trail.

Location
Hernando, Hillsborough, Pasco

Endpoints
Upper Tampa Bay Trail at W. Lutz Lake Fern Road at Suncoast Pkwy./ FL 589 (Keystone) to US 98/W. Ponce De Leon Blvd., 0.4 mile northwest of FL 589/Suncoast Pkwy. (Brooksville)

Mileage
42

Type
Greenway/Non-Rail-Trail

Roughness Index
1

Surface
Asphalt

longleaf pine forests and palm groves bring you to a trail intersection with the Starkey Park Bike Trail; this paved trail heads west 6.5 miles through the Starkey Wilderness Park. Five-and-a-half more miles of trail with similar forest and lowland scenes will bring you to FL 52 and another major road crossing.

The next 11 miles of trail traverse a landscape of mainly sparse, rural homesteads and agricultural plots. Cattle, horses, goats, and even donkeys keep you company along this stretch, which bridges the line between Pasco and Hernando Counties. Less than 2 miles north of County Line Road, you will reach a short connector trail to Anderson Snow Park, a large park complex that serves as a primary trailhead and parking area for the trail. Mixtures of suburban residential areas and open scrubland permeate the next 6 miles until you come to another well-developed trailhead (south of Cortez Boulevard) with water, restrooms, and parking.

The last 12 miles of the Suncoast boast one final surprise: hills. After miles upon miles of classic Florida flatland, you get the opportunity to use your gears. Although they are not mountainous climbs, they are noticeable after almost 30 miles of flat riding.

CONTACT: tinyurl.com/suncoasttrl

DIRECTIONS

To reach the southern trailhead from I-75, take Exit 275 for FL 56. Head west on FL 56, and drive 5.1 miles as the road changes to FL 54. Turn left onto Land O' Lakes Blvd., and in 0.3 mile turn right onto Dale Mabry Hwy. Head south on Dale Mabry Hwy. 2.3 miles, and then turn right onto W. Lutz Lake Fern Road. After 3.6 miles, look for the trailhead on the right (by Suncoast Pkwy.).

To reach the FL 54 trailhead from I-75, take Exit 275 for FL 56. Head west on FL 56, and drive 10.4 miles as the road changes to FL 54. Just west of Suncoast Pkwy., the trailhead is on the north side. Turn right into an access road across from Crossings Blvd. to the trailhead.

To reach the Anderson Snow Park trailhead from I-75, take Exit 285 for FL 52 toward Dade City. Head west on FL 52, and go 14 miles. Turn right onto FL 589/Suncoast Pkwy. (toll road), and in 8.3 miles take Exit 37 for County Line Road. Turn left onto County Line Road, and in 0.4 mile turn right onto Anderson Snow Road. In 1.7 miles the park will be on the east side of the road.

To reach the northern trailhead from I-75, take Exit 301 for US 98/FL 50 toward Brooksville. Head west on US 98/FL 50, and in 10.7 miles turn right onto US 98/Ponce De Leon Blvd. After 12.1 miles, the trailhead will be on the southwest side of the road.

Be advised that all trailheads along the Suncoast Trail have a $2/car parking fee.

Tallahassee–St. Marks Historic Railroad State Trail follows the route of the state's first and longest-operating railroad, created in the mid-1800s to transport cotton from plantations to awaiting ships at Port Leon, near the Gulf of Mexico.

Today, St. Marks Trail (also the first paved trail in the state) offers 20.5 miles of adventure along a variety of urban and more remote environments, passing side trails and state parks along the way. Longleaf pines and forests of oak, wax myrtle, and yaupon holly shade the route.

The best place to begin your journey is the Capital Circle trailhead (on Woodville Highway south of Capital

The northern section of the St. Marks Trail offers a smooth ride underneath a thick canopy of trees.

Location
Leon, Wakulla

Endpoints
Gamble St. and Stearns St. (Tallahassee) to Riverside Drive (St. Marks)

Mileage
20.5

Type
Rail-Trail

Roughness Index
1

Surface
Asphalt

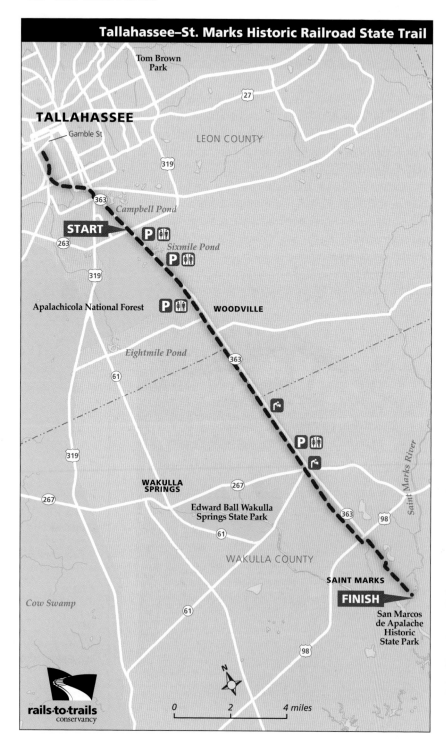

Tallahassee–St. Marks Historic Railroad State Trail

Circle), which provides ample parking and restrooms for trail users. Heading north 4.5 miles to the trail's endpoint takes you several blocks away from Florida State University and the Stadium Drive Bikepath, which is frequented by students. Note that the first few miles south of the endpoint can be a bit congested, particularly on the weekends.

If you are riding a mountain bike, consider exploring the Munson Hills Off-Road Trail, located 1 mile south (mileage is painted on the asphalt) of the Capital Circle trailhead; look for the entrance to the right, across from Longevity Lane. The loop system can get sandy during dry months, but the scenic areas and remote terrain make it worth a visit. Wakulla Station trailhead, near mile 9, provides water, shelter, and restrooms. A bit farther south, you can take a 5-mile detour along the paved shoulder of FL 267 to get to Wakulla Springs State Park, known for its big, beautiful spring and a refreshing swimming hole.

At the trail's southern terminus is the city of St. Marks, which boasts small waterfront restaurants and views of cruising boats on the St. Marks River. To the south and west of the trail's end is the 500,000-acre San Marcos de Apalache Historic State Park, which features longleaf pines, native grasses, wildflowers, and rare animals, including the largest concentration of red-cockaded woodpeckers in the world.

CONTACT: floridastateparks.org/trail/tallahassee-st-marks

DIRECTIONS

To reach the Capital Circle trailhead from I-10, take Exit 199 for US 27 toward Havana/Tallahassee/State Capitol (0.5 mile). Head south on US 27/N. Monroe St. (signs for Tallahassee), and go 8.1 miles (after 3.8 miles, the road becomes S. Monroe St., and in another 2.5 miles, it becomes FL 363 S.). The destination will be on the right. The address of the trailhead is 4778 Woodville Hwy.

Trail access and ample parking are available at the Woodville Park and Recreation Complex. From I-10, take Exit 199 for US 27 toward Havana/Tallahassee/State Capitol (0.5 mile). Head south on US 27/N. Monroe St. (signs for Tallahassee), and go 10.6 miles (after 3.8 miles, the road becomes S. Monroe St., and in another 2.5 miles, it becomes FL 363 S.). Turn right onto Old Woodville Road, and continue 0.3 mile. Turn right into the complex at Back Forest Road.

Wakulla Station trailhead is located off FL 363/Woodville Hwy., just south of the Leon–Wakulla county line. To reach the trailhead from I-10, take Exit 199 for US 27 toward Havana/Tallahassee/State Capitol (0.5 mile). Head south on US 27/N. Monroe St. (signs for Tallahassee), and go 24 miles (after 3.8 miles, the road becomes S. Monroe St., and in another 2.5 miles, it becomes FL 363 S.). Turn right onto Riverside Drive; look for parking on your right. (Look for brown directional signs to the trailhead from FL 363.)

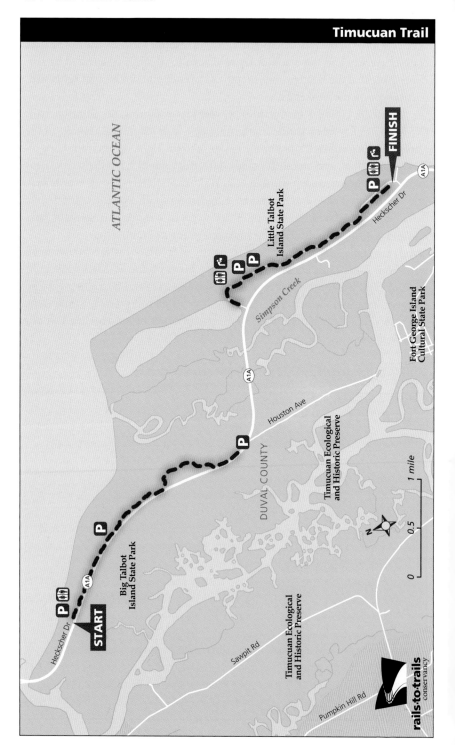

The 4.8-mile Timucuan Trail is composed of northern and southern segments that are divided by a short on-road segment on FL A1A, crossing Simpson Creek and the sloughs of Timucuan Ecological and Historic Preserve.

The northern segment of the Timucuan Trail is similar to its northern sister, the Amelia Island Trail (see page 8). Floridian fauna are on full display, and the hot and humid temperatures remind riders to hydrate frequently and escape to the shade when possible. The Timucuan Ecological and Historic Preserve flanks the trail and beckons trail users to explore the region around the path. Bird enthusiasts will be excited to learn that the brilliantly colorful painted bunting calls the preserve home.

The southern segment of the Timucuan Trail runs through Little Talbot Island State Park. Most of the trail is adjacent to the road leading into the park; the trail shares

The junglelike foliage in the northern section of the Timucuan Trail (which changes to desertlike dunes as you head south)

Location
Duval

Endpoints
Big Talbot Island State Park at FL A1A, 0.9 mile south of George Crady Bridge, to Little Talbot Island State Park at FL A1A, 0.75 mile north of bridge over Fort George River Inlet (Jacksonville)

Mileage
4.8

Type
Greenway/Non-Rail-Trail

Roughness Index
1

Surface
Asphalt

this road for most of its length. There are many opportunities to access the beach along the route, and the park offers bike rentals at the entrance station.

As the trail continues south along the road, the landscape changes from dense, junglelike foliage to windblown, desertlike dunes. The trail is also part of the East Coast Greenway.

CONTACT: **timucuantrailparksfoundation.org**

DIRECTIONS

To reach the northern trailhead at Big Talbot Island State Park from I-95, take Exit 373 for FL 200/FL A1A. Head east on FL 200/FL A1A, and drive 11.2 miles. Turn right onto Amelia Island Pkwy., and follow the road 2.5 miles. Turn right onto Buccaneer Trail; continue on Buccaneer Trail 1.2 miles, and then continue straight at the traffic circle onto FL A1A S. Go 7 miles, passing through three more traffic circles and over the Nassau River and Sawpit Creek to Big Talbot Island State Park. Turn left into the parking area.

To reach the southern trailhead at Little Talbot Island State Park from I-295, take Exit 41 for FL 105 N., and head east on FL 105/Hecksher Drive. Go 14 miles, traveling along the St. Johns River toward the Atlantic Coast (FL 105 becomes FL A1A as you cross Clapboard Creek near Batten Island). Turn right onto the access road. (You'll pass several parking lots for trail access to the northern endpoint of this trail segment.) Continue on the access road 2 miles; the southern trailhead and parking lot are located on the right where the access road reunites with FL A1A.

Widely regarded as one of Tampa Bay's best suburban trails, the Upper Tampa Bay Trail provides a scenic escape from its congested surroundings. The original section winds through Town 'n' Country along the west bank of the Channel A drainage canal before entering residential Citrus Park, where it joins an unused railroad corridor, while a newer, non-rail-trail segment links trail users with the 42-mile Suncoast Trail farther north. From the Old Memorial trailhead, the original section of the trail extends north, wedged between Channel A and Montague Street. Less than a half mile in, a convenient connection to Braulio Alonso High School serves commuting students. At West Waters Avenue, you have the option of crossing

The Upper Tampa Bay Trail provides a scenic escape from its congested surroundings with native vegetation and trees to line the way.

Location
Hillsborough

Endpoints
Old Memorial trailhead at Memorial Hwy. and Montague St. (Town 'n' Country) to Suncoast Trail at W. Lutz Lake Fern Road at Suncoast Pkwy./ FL 589 (Keystone)

Mileage
12.1

Type
Rail-Trail

Roughness Index
1

Surface
Asphalt

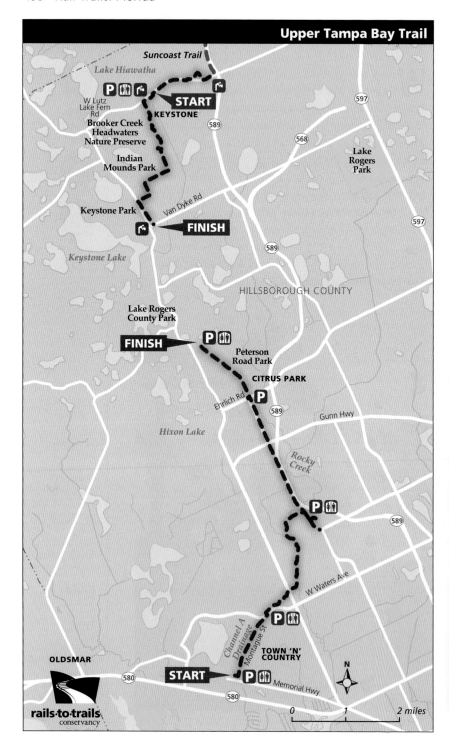

Upper Tampa Bay Trail

Suncoast Trail

Lake Hiawatha

W Lutz
Lake Fern
Rd

START

KEYSTONE

Brooker Creek
Headwaters
Nature Preserve

Indian
Mounds Park

589

597

568

Lake
Rogers
Park

Keystone Park

Van Dyke Rd

FINISH

597

Keystone Lake

589

HILLSBOROUGH COUNTY

Lake Rogers
County Park

FINISH

Peterson
Road Park

CITRUS PARK

Ehrlich Rd

589

Gunn Hwy

Hixon Lake

Rocky
Creek

589

W Waters Ave

Channel A
Drainage

Montague St

TOWN 'N'
COUNTRY

OLDSMAR

580

START

580

Memorial Hwy

N

rails·to·trails
conservancy

0   1   2 miles

the busy road at-grade or below, closer to the waterway. Eventually, you'll reach the Channel Park trailhead, which offers plenty of parking, restrooms, and an information center.

The route turns sharply northeast from the trailhead and continues to follow the Channel A waterway to where it meets peaceful Rocky Creek. This scenic stretch is lined with native vegetation and beautiful cypress trees. At a quaint wooden trail bridge over the creek, you'll leave the waterway, turning north to follow Veterans Expressway/FL 589. At busy Gunn Highway, you're transported over the road on a beautifully constructed trail bridge. North of here, the trail picks up the former railroad corridor and continues arrow-straight past Ehrlich Road. Local eateries dot the road; through-travelers should be sure to cross at the nearby Gunn Highway traffic light to avoid a treacherous (and illegal) crossing of the busy four-lane road. The final mile of this segment to Peterson Road Park becomes increasingly rural, with grazing cattle, sheep, and other livestock occasionally making appearances.

A gap just longer than a mile currently separates the original portion of the Upper Tampa Bay Trail from the newest section, completed in 2015. Pick up the new northern stretch at its only trailhead with parking on West Lutz Lake Fern Road. This massive trailhead also offers restrooms and water and is a popular stop for people on the nearby Suncoast Trail.

Continue east from the trailhead along West Lutz Lake Fern Road to reach the southern endpoint of the Suncoast Trail at Suncoast Parkway (FL 589). You'll pass over two long, low bridges over swampland and wind through a small forest before reaching the trail junction. (Note: Those familiar with the Suncoast Trail should be aware that the trailhead at the intersection of West Lutz Lake Fern Road and Suncoast Parkway has been removed in favor of the larger facility farther west.) Back at the new trailhead, head southwest on smooth pavement to access the majority of the newer northern segment through the scenic Brooker Creek Headwaters Nature Preserve. The serpentine route was built close to the ground for environmental reasons, but this means it is prone to flooding; standing water is a common sight and minor obstacle. Several hiking-only, natural-surface trails (with bike racks) branch off from the paved trail throughout this stretch, providing opportunities to explore the preserve.

Just before reaching the segment's southern endpoint across from a grocery store, the trail's surroundings transition from swampland to pastoral farmland. In the near future, the trail will extend south to meet the older portion of trail at Peterson Park.

CONTACT: hillsboroughcounty.org/facilities

DIRECTIONS

To reach the Old Memorial trailhead from the intersection of I-275 and FL 589, head north on FL 589 (toll road). Drive 3.4 miles to Exit 4 for W. Hillsborough Ave./FL 580. Turn left onto W. Hillsborough Ave., and head west 4.8 miles to Montague St. Turn right, and go 0.4 mile. Turn right on Memorial Hwy. The trailhead is on the right in 0.4 mile.

To reach Peterson Road Park from the intersection of I-275 and FL 589, head north on FL 589 (toll road). Drive 10.6 miles to Exit 10 for Ehrlich Road. Turn left, head west 1 mile, and turn right onto Gunn Highway. Drive 1.1 miles north on Gunn Highway, and turn right onto Peterson Road. The trailhead is in the park to your left.

To reach the trailhead on W. Lutz Lake Fern Road from the intersection of I-275 and FL 589, head north on FL 589 (toll road). Drive 12.9 miles to Exit 16 for W. Lutz Lake Fern Road, and turn right. Continue west on W. Lutz Lake Fern Road 1.5 miles to the trailhead on the left, just beyond Angel Lane. To reach the trailhead from I-75, take Exit 275 for FL 56. Head west on FL 56, and drive 5.1 miles as the road changes to FL 54. Turn left onto Land O' Lakes Blvd., and in 0.3 mile turn right onto Dale Mabry Hwy. Head south on Dale Mabry Hwy. 2.3 miles, and then turn right onto W. Lutz Lake Fern Road. After 4.7 miles, look for the trailhead on the left, just past Angel Lane.

The Waldo Road Greenway, Depot Avenue Rail-Trail, and Kermit Sigmon Bike Trail have been seamlessly connected as part of Gainesville's ever-expanding rail-trail network. Together, the three comprise a 6.4-mile network that links neighborhoods, businesses, transit stops, a private aviation terminal, and the University of Florida campus. They connect with the new 6th Street Rail Trail extension and will soon connect with the scenic Gainesville–Hawthorne State Trail at Depot Park (see page 56). While there are no formal trailheads or parking areas, you can access the route from a number of road crossings. (Depot Park and the Old Gainesville Depot are being restored to serve as a formal trailhead.) Starting from the north at Waldo Road and Northeast 47th

The popular commuter network links neighborhoods, transit stops, and community destinations, as well as the University of Florida campus.

Location
Alachua

Endpoints
N.E. Waldo Road and N.E. 47th Ave. to FL 24/S.W. Archer Road and FL 24A/S.W. 16th Ave. (Gainesville)

Mileage
6.4

Type
Rail-Trail

Roughness Index
1

Surface
Asphalt, Concrete

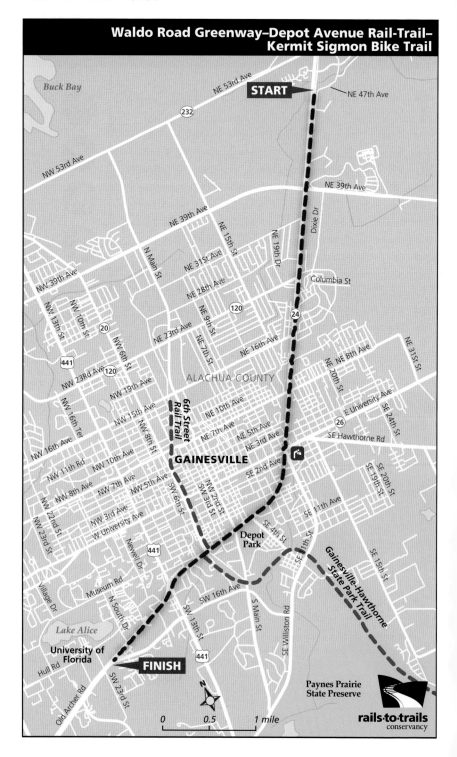

Waldo Road Greenway–Depot Avenue Rail-Trail–Kermit Sigmon Bike Trail

Buck Bay

START

NE 53rd Ave

NE 47th Ave

232

NW 53rd Ave

NE 39th Ave

Dixie Dr

NE 39th Ave

NE 15th St

N Main St

NE 31st Ave

NE 19th Dr

Columbia St

NW 39th Ave

NE 28th Ave

NW 13th St

NW 10th St

NE 23rd Ave

NE 9th St

120

24

NE 7th St

NE 16th Ave

NE 8th Ave

20

NW 6th St

NE 20th St

NE 31st St

441

120

NW 23rd Ave

ALACHUA COUNTY

E University Ave

SE 24th St

NW 16th Ave

NW 19th Ave

6th Street Rail Trail

NE 10th Ave

26

SE Hawthorne Rd

NW 15th Ave

NW 8th St

NE 7th Ave

NE 5th Ave

SE 20th St

SE 19th St

NW 16th Ave

NW 11th Rd

NW 10th Ave

GAINESVILLE

NE 3rd Ave

SE 2nd Ave

NW 8th Ave

NW 7th Ave

NW 5th Ave

NW 2nd St

NW 3rd St

NW 3rd Ave

W University Ave

SW 6th St

SW 11th Ave

NW 22nd St

Depot Park

SE 4th St

SE 11th Ave

Gainesville-Hawthorne State Park Trail

NW 23rd St

Newell Dr

441

Museum Rd

SW 16th Ave

S Main St

SE Williston Rd

SE 15th St

Village Dr

Lake Alice

N South Dr

SW 13th St

University of Florida

FINISH

441

Paynes Prairie State Preserve

Hull Rd

Old Archer Rd

SW 23rd St

N

0   0.5   1 mile

rails·to·trails
conservancy

Avenue, the Waldo Road Greenway is particularly well landscaped and passes numerous public transportation connections. Be aware that the trail narrows at intersections and at a few of the transit stops.

The Depot Avenue Rail-Trail picks up across the street on the west side of Southeast 11th Street at the Waldo Road/University Avenue intersection and threads through local neighborhoods. Along the route, you will find Depot Park, bounded at the north by the Old Gainesville Depot, which is listed on the National Register of Historic Places. The depot was in continuous use from 1907 until the 1930s, when a new passenger depot building in town replaced it. In a nod to Gainesville's history as a hub for passenger and freight rails, a section of the old railroad tracks can also be seen adjacent to the depot building. Across from Depot Park is the Rosa Parks Regional Transit Downtown Station for bus connections; most buses are fitted with front bike racks.

A few blocks farther along at the intersection of Southwest Depot Avenue and Southwest Sixth Street, the trail connects north to the 6th Street Rail Trail, which extends about 1.7 miles and ends at Northwest 16th Avenue. Continuing west, you will pass by the University of Florida campus and over the 13th Street Bridge, which boasts an award-winning, renovated helix trestle structure.

Across the trestle, you'll join the Kermit Sigmon Bike Trail. Named for a local doctor, the trail leads west past both Shands and Veterans Hospitals and is a popular commuting corridor for hospital employees. Although the route continues another 2 miles west, it's recommended that you end your trip here; the Archer Road crossing farther on poses a significant hazard, as its narrow sidewalk flanks the wrong side of the road for westbound cyclists.

CONTACT: **gainesvillepublicworks.org**

DIRECTIONS

While there are no formal parking areas or trailheads, the route offers numerous access points, particularly along Waldo and Archer Roads, where the trail intersects with S.W. 13th and S. Main Sts., and on several side streets.

To reach the northern endpoint from I-75, take Exit 390 for FL 222 toward Gainesville. Head east on FL 222/N.W. 39th Ave., and drive 9.4 miles. Turn left onto FL 24/N.E. Waldo Road, and go 1 mile. The trail ends where FL 24/N.E. Waldo Road intersects with N.E. 47th Ave.

To reach the southern endpoint from I-75, take Exit 384 toward Gainesville. Head east on FL 24/S.W. Archer Road, and go 2.5 miles. The trail begins where FL 24/S.W. Archer Road intersects with FL 24A/S.W. 16th Ave.

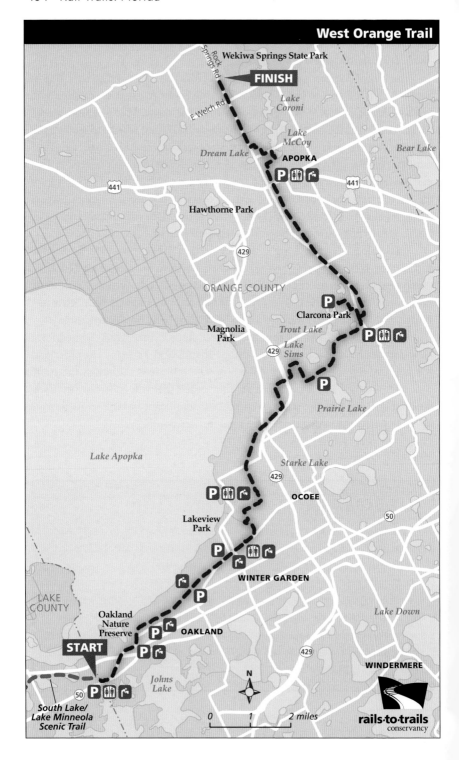

Lined by Spanish moss–draped oaks and meandering around lakes and through fields and the charming town of Winter Garden, the West Orange Trail is one of Florida's most popular rail-trails. This diverse pathway connects small communities and suburban neighborhoods yet offers ample opportunities for viewing wildlife along the way. The trail is wide, well maintained, and dotted with several trailhead stations and outposts with parking, water, and other amenities.

Fifteen minutes northwest of downtown Orlando, the West Orange Trail serves as a window on the region's past and present, passing through 1950s communities that grew up around the once-thriving Orange Belt Railway, as well as more-developed areas in this rapidly expanding metropolitan area. The pathway currently stretches 22 miles from Oakland to Apopka but will eventually continue north into Lake County for a total of 36 miles. Killarney Station,

Parking, water, and other amenities dot the well-maintained West Orange Trail.

Location
Orange

Endpoints
South Lake and Lake Minneola Scenic Trail at Killarney Station at Old County Road 50/FL 438 and Lake Blvd. (Oakland) to E. Lester Road and Rock Springs Road/FL 435 (Apopka)

Mileage
22

Type
Rail-Trail

Roughness Index
1

Surface
Asphalt, Concrete, Dirt, Wood Chips

a modern take on an old-time train depot, anchors the southern trailhead and serves as the eastern trailhead of the South Lake and Lake Minneola Scenic Trail. Here you'll find bike rentals, restrooms, parking, and water.

From Killarney Station, the route leads northeast, passing the Oakland Nature Preserve and the quiet, wooded community of Oakland before hitting downtown Winter Garden. For about a mile, the trail threads down the middle of two-lane Plant Street, allowing trail users to browse the shops, markets, and restaurants of this lively community. The trail passes near Winter Garden's Downtown Pavilion, where a bustling Saturday open-air market greets locals and tourists alike. Other attractions include the Central Florida Railroad Museum and the Winter Garden Heritage Museum.

For the next 10 miles, the trail pops in and out of thinly wooded areas, occasionally passing orange groves that speak to the county's agricultural roots. This stretch is open to equestrian use along a side path and connects to Clarcona Horseman's Park. The trail continues through suburban neighborhoods and roadways to Apopka, one of Central Florida's fastest growing communities. You'll soon cross busy US 441 along Forest Avenue. The trail runs 3 more miles along North Park Avenue before ending at the current northernmost trailhead on East Welch Road.

CONTACT: orangecountyfl.net/CultureParks

DIRECTIONS

To reach the Killarney Station trailhead from I-4, take Exit 77 toward Ocala (partial toll road), and merge onto Florida's Turnpike (toll road), heading northwest. Drive 12.6 miles, and take Exit 272 toward Clermont. Merge onto FL 50 W./W. Colonial Drive. Follow FL 50 W. 1.4 miles, and turn right onto Lake Blvd. After 0.2 mile, turn right onto FL 438 S./Old County Road 50 E. Immediately turn right into the trailhead.

To reach the Winter Garden trailhead from I-4, take Exit 82A, and merge onto FL 408, heading west. Drive 9.4 miles, and take the Florida's Turnpike exit toward Ocala. Head north on Florida's Turnpike (toll road), and continue on the road 1.3 miles. Take Exit 267A to FL 429 N./Apopka. Merge onto FL 429 N. (toll road), and go 0.2 mile. Take Exit 24, and head west on FL 438/Plant St. After 1.4 miles, the trailhead will be to your right. For parking, take Plant St. less than 0.5 mile farther; public parking is available along the street, to your right.

To reach the Apopka trailhead, take I-4 to Exit 83A or 84 for FL 50/W. Colonial Drive, and head west 0.9 mile. Turn right onto US 441, and drive north 11.4 miles to County Road 435/S. Park Ave. Turn right onto CR 435/S. Park Ave., and look for the trailhead 2.3 miles ahead on the right, where CR 435 and E. Welch Road intersect. While there is no parking at this trailhead, you can park along the route.

Withlacoochee Bay Trail, while not lengthy, is a stunningly beautiful trail to ride that packs a punch into a shorter trail. With top-notch views of the Withlacoochee barge channel on one side and expansive Florida marshland to the south, trail users find themselves stopping regularly to enjoy the scenery. The trail's flat, well-maintained asphalt surface makes it accessible to all skill levels. The stunning view of the Gulf at the western terminus punctuates a truly outstanding Florida trail experience. From its eastern terminus, this trail traverses 6 miles along the shipping canal of the Withlacoochee River. Wildlife abounds, and common sightings include snakes, armadillos, turtles, wild turkeys, numerous bird species, and even dolphins and alligators at the western end.

The trail is a smooth asphalt ride with little elevation, making for a nice, simple experience for all skill sets.

An access road leads to the Withlacoochee Bay Trail's more remote trailheads, as well as fishing areas and a large equestrian area.

Location
Citrus

Endpoints
0.4 mile east of US 19/US 98 at Cross Florida Barge Channel to 4.2 miles west of US 19/US 98 at the Gulf of Mexico (Inglis)

Mileage
6.2

Type
Greenway/Non-Rail-Trail

Roughness Index
1

Surface
Asphalt

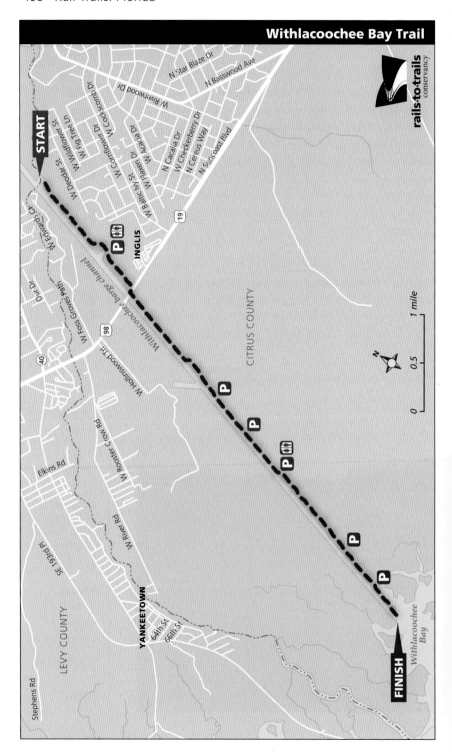

Withlacoochee Bay Trail

Multiple parking areas and trailheads offer ample opportunities for accessing the trail, as well as restroom stops for trail users.

To the south of the trail, an expansive equestrian park caters to riding enthusiasts. Dotted throughout the trail are observation decks offering enticing places to rest and enjoy the sights of the canal, the amazing marshlands to the south, or, at the end, the Gulf of Mexico. While the trail and trailheads close at dark, you might want to time your trip to catch just a bit of a Gulf sunset at the western terminus before heading back east.

If you're up for a longer challenge, don't miss the Withlacoochee State Trail (see page 170), located just a few miles east of the eastern terminus of the Withlacoochee Bay Trail.

CONTACT: **floridastateparks.org/trail/Cross-Withlacoochee**

DIRECTIONS

To reach the western trailhead near the Gulf of Mexico from I-75, take Exit 352 for FL 40/Silver Springs Blvd. Head west on FL 40/Silver Springs Blvd., and drive 17.3 miles. Turn left onto US 41, and go 4.1 miles. Turn right onto Powell Road, and in 0.5 mile turn right onto Cedar St., which soon becomes FL 40/Orlando St. Go 13.2 miles, and turn left onto US 19/US 98. In 1.8 miles turn right onto the gravel access road, and go 4.6 miles to the parking area.

To reach parking at the barge channel trailhead, follow the directions above, but turn left onto the access road on the east side of the highway, and drive 0.8 mile until you reach the parking lot directly ahead.

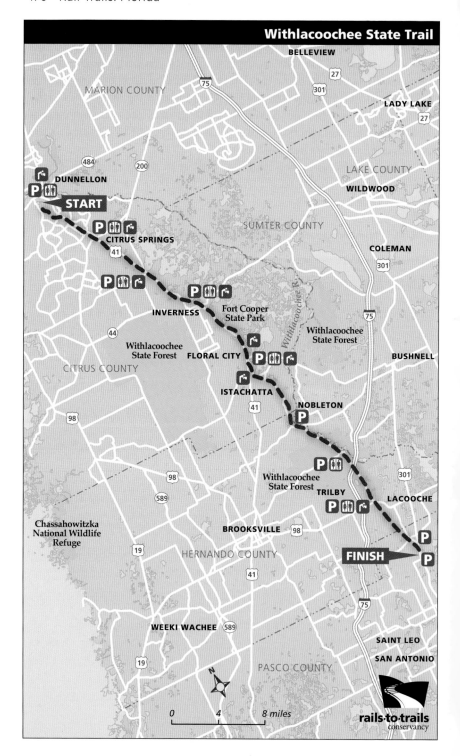

Withlacoochee State Trail

At 46 miles, the Withlacoochee State Trail is one of the longest paved pathways in the state, offering a quintessential Florida experience as it travels through a variety of terrains and environs. With a primarily flat terrain, smooth surface, and numerous access points, the trail is the perfect venue for biking, walking, jogging, or skating and provides a maintained, separate horse treadway alongside the trail.

Starting in Citrus County at the northern end, the trail begins its journey south through wooded deciduous forests, with the occasional palm, many ferns, and some shade. You'll notice railroad markers on the side, a remnant of the corridor's past, marking the mileage to Richmond, Virginia, along what was the region's main line north. The trail is more remote than many of the area's other trails, making for a peaceful experience.

The Withlacoochee State Trail provides a remote and peaceful experience for trail users.

Location
Citrus, Hernando, Pasco

Endpoints
Magenta Drive and W. Shellbark Drive (Dunnellon) to US 301 just south of Mickler Road (Lacoochee)

Mileage
46

Type
Rail-Trail

Roughness Index
1

Surface
Asphalt, Concrete

The Withlacoochee's length, popularity, and proximity to numerous communities have given rise to numerous trailheads, information kiosks, colorful murals, and convenient parks. Food and drink are never too far away as you travel south through Citrus Springs, Inverness, Floral City, Istachatta, and Trilby.

For much of its length, the trail parallels the Withlacoochee River, a state-designated paddling trail. The best place to catch river views and put in your canoe or kayak is at Nobleton Wayside Park, about 8 miles south of Floral City. From here, the trail crosses the Withlacoochee State Forest and Croom Wildlife Management Area. Expect to see deer in the mornings and early evenings along this roughly 6-mile stretch. Near the southern boundary, Silver Lake Recreation Area offers year-round camping.

Around mile 16, the town of Inverness provides good trail access, as well as food and lodging. Inverness is just north of the trail's most expansive water and wildlife views (there are also boardwalks and interpretive signs). As you make your way along the trail, be sure to fill up your water bottles, get enough nourishment, and take advantage of shady areas as the trail is exposed to the sun in certain areas, particularly during the summer months. The modest distances between trailheads and towns can seem remote and wild. With upland forests at the north end of the trail and wetland swamps at the south end, the trail is never too far from an abundance of Florida wildlife. Keep an eye out for hawks, waterfowl, deer, and the occasional reptile.

The trail is bounded by ferns, evergreens, and hardwood trees throughout its entirety, with occasional glimpses of the river in between. The Spanish moss and live oaks are a friendly reminder of your location in the coastal South, where it's not uncommon to share the trail with a wild turkey or have your presence noted by a hooting owl in the canopy above.

CONTACT: **floridastateparks.org/trail/withlacoochee** or **railstotrailsonline.com**

DIRECTIONS

To reach the Gulf Junction trailhead from I-75, take Exit 329 for FL 44 toward Inverness/Wildwood. Head west on FL 44, and drive 14.9 miles. Turn right onto US 41, and in 1 mile turn right to remain on US 41. In 15.1 miles turn left onto W. G. Martinelli Blvd. After 0.5 mile, turn left onto N. Haitian Drive, and continue 0.2 mile. Turn right onto W. Shellbark Drive, and continue 0.3 mile. Passing over W. Magenta Drive, the road curves right to the trailhead and parking.

To reach the South Citrus Springs trailhead from I-75, take Exit 329 for FL 44 toward Inverness/Wildwood. Head west on FL 44, and drive 14.9 miles. Turn right onto US 41, and in 1 mile turn right to remain on US 41. In 11.5 miles turn left onto S. Citrus Springs Blvd., and head west one block. The trailhead is on the left.

To reach the Inverness trailhead from I-75, take Exit 329 for FL 44 toward Inverness/Wildwood. Head west on FL 44, and drive 14.9 miles. Turn right onto US 41, and in 0.4 mile turn right onto Courthouse Square. Then make an immediate right onto N. Apopka Ave. The marked trailhead is 0.3 mile up N. Apopka Ave.

To reach the Ridge Manor trailhead, take I-75 to Exit 301 for US 98 S./FL 50 E., and head east on FL 50 E./US 98 S. After about 1 mile, turn left onto Croom Rital Road, and look for the trailhead on the right after 0.3 mile.

To reach the Trilby trailhead from I-75, take Exit 301 for US 98 S./FL 50 E. Head east on FL 50 E./US 98 S./Cortez Blvd., and drive 3 miles. Turn right onto US 98 S./McKethan Road, and continue 3.1 miles. Turn right onto Trilby Road. Turn right into the trailhead, just before Trilby Cutoff Road.

To reach the Owensboro Junction trailhead from I-75, take Exit 301 for US 98 S./FL 50 E. Head east on FL 50 E./US 98 S./Cortez Blvd., and drive 3 miles. Turn right onto US 98 S./McKethan Road, and continue 3.9 miles. Make a slight right onto US 301 S./US 98 S., and drive 0.6 mile. Turn right into the trailhead and parking.

Index

Opposite: *The 106.5-mile Florida Keys Overseas Heritage Trail features the unmatched beauty of the Atlantic Ocean and Gulf of Mexico. (see page 46).*

Photo Credits

Page iii: Eli Griffen; *page iv:* Milo Bateman; *page viii:* Laura Stark; *page x:* Milo Bateman; *page 7:* Milo Bateman; *page 9:* Katie Harris; *page 11:* Ken Bryan; *page 15:* Jim Brown; *page 17:* Milo Bateman; *page 21:* John Moran, courtesy of the Florida Department of Environmental Protection; *page 23:* Ken Bryan; *page 27:* Brian Gerhardstein; *page 29:* Milo Bateman; *page 33:* Jim Brown; *page 35:* Ryan Cree; *page 39:* Jonathan Rayer; *page 43:* Jonathan Rayer; *page 47:* Milo Bateman; *page 49:* Jim Brown; *page 53:* Jim Brown; *page 57:* Katie Harris; *page 59:* Jonathan Rayer; *page 63:* Brian Gerhardstein; *page 65:* Ryan Cree; *page 69:* Katie Harris; *page 71:* Laura Stark; *page 75:* Jonathan Rayer; *page 77:* Jonathan Rayer; *page 81:* Brian Gerhardstein; *page 83:* Leeann Sinpatanasakul; *page 87:* Jonathan Rayer; *page 89:* Milo Bateman; *page 93:* John Moran, courtesy of the Florida Department of Environmental Protection; *page 95:* Barry Bergman; *page 99:* Jim Brown; *page 103:* Barry Bergman; *page 105:* Milo Bateman; *page 109:* Anya Saretzky; *page 111:* Katie Harris; *page 115:* Milo Bateman; *page 117:* Eli Griffen; *page 121:* Ken Bryan; *page 125:* Jonathan Rayer; *page 127:* Brian Gerhardstein; *page 131:* Jonathan Rayer; *page 135:* Ken Bryan; *page 137:* Milo Bateman; *page 141:* Milo Bateman; *page 145:* Ken Bryan; *page 149:* Eric Oberg; *page 151:* Doug Alderson; *page 155:* Katie Harris; *page 157:* Eli Griffen; *page 161:* Leeann Sinpatanasakul; *page 165:* Ryan Cree; *page 167:* Eric Oberg; *page 171:* Jim Brown; *page 178:* Milo Bateman.

Support Rails-to-Trails Conservancy

The nation's leader in helping communities transform unused rail lines and connecting corridors into multiuse trails, Rails-to-Trails Conservancy (RTC) depends on the support of its members and donors to create access to healthy outdoor experiences.

Your donation will help support programs and services that have helped put more than 22,000 rail-trail miles on the ground. Every day, RTC provides vital assistance to communities to develop and maintain trails throughout the country. In addition, RTC advocates for trail-friendly policies, promotes the benefits of rail-trails, and defends rail-trail laws in the courts.

Join online at **railstotrails.org,** or mail your donation to Rails-to-Trails Conservancy, 2121 Ward Court N.W., Fifth Floor, Washington, D.C. 20037.

Rails-to-Trails Conservancy is a 501(c)(3) nonprofit organization, and contributions are tax deductible.